God's Truth About the End of Time

Arnold Johnson

WestBow
PRESS
A DIVISION OF THOMAS NELSON

WestBow Press books may be ordered through booksellers or by contacting:

WestBow Press
A Division of Thomas Nelson
1663 Liberty Drive
Bloomington, IN 47403
www.westbowpress.com
1-(866) 928-1240

ISBN: 978-1-4497-1294-5 (sc)
ISBN: 978-1-4497-1296-9 (hc)
ISBN: 978-1-4497-1295-2 (e)

Library of Congress Control Number: 2011922935

Scripture taken from the King James Version of the Holy Bible.

Printed in the United States of America
WestBow Press rev. date: 2/23/2011

PART 1:
GOD'S TRUTH ABOUT THE END OF TIME

Truth, what is truth? One man's truth can be another man's lie. It all depends on your point of view. But man's truth is not what we are going to study here. The events of the end of the world are God's design and God's truth, and this is what you will find here. What follows is what the Bible tells us about the end of time as we know it.

The best place to start this study is with the Book of Revelation. Many know that this book shows us how the world will end, but it is such a mysterious and hard to read book that most do not attempt to understand it. This book is meant to be understood, and it is my goal that you will have a complete understanding of this book by the time you finish this work.

There are those who have studied the writings of this book, and offered varying opinions and beliefs on how to interpret it. For the most part, these interpretations believe that this time period is just senseless destruction from a vengeful God, but we will discover that it is much more. For these events that take place are what make it possible for us to go to heaven. And until these events take place, and in the proper order, we will not be able to go to heaven and stand before God.

Understanding the New Testament

The beginning of the end of time was initiated by Jesus, when he came to earth as the Lamb of God. Yes, Jesus came to earth to save us by taking our sins upon his body, but this is not the complete story. Jesus also fulfilled the Old Testament and brought us the New Testament, which must still be fulfilled. Few understand what this means, but to understand the Book of Revelation, it is necessary to have a basic understanding of what Jesus did for us concerning the Testaments.

The Old Testament is the First Covenant

The first covenant had ordinances of divine service, and a worldly sanctuary. The first part of the tabernacle was the sanctuary, which held

1

the candlestick, table, and showbread. The second part of the tabernacle was behind the veil, and was called the Holiest of all. It held the golden censer and the Ark of the Covenant, overlaid with gold. Inside the Ark of the Covenant are the golden pot that has manna, Aaron's rod that budded, and the tables of the covenant. Over the ark are the cherubim's of glory, shadowing the mercy seat; of which we cannot now speak particularly. Hebrews 9:1-5

Now when these things were ordained, the priests always went into the first tabernacle, accomplishing the service of God. But only the high priest went into the second part, alone, just once every year. And only with blood, which he offered for himself, and for the errors of the people. The Holy Ghost thus showing, that the way into the holiest of all was not yet made manifest, while as the first tabernacle was yet standing. Hebrews 9:6-8

The first tabernacle was a figure for the present time, where gifts and sacrifices were offered, that could not make those who performed the service perfect, as pertaining to the conscience. It stood only in meats and drinks, various washings, and carnal ordinances, which were imposed on them until the time of reformation. Hebrews 9:9-10

The New Testament is the Second Covenant

But Christ became the High Priest of good things to come, with a greater and more perfect tabernacle, not made with hands, that is to say, not of this building. He entered once into the holy place, not with the blood of goats and calves, but with his own blood, after having obtained eternal redemption for us. Hebrews 9:11-12

The blood of bulls and goats, and the ashes of a heifer sprinkling the unclean, sanctifies to the purifying of the flesh. But the blood of Christ, who through the eternal Spirit offered himself without spot to God, purges your conscience from dead works to serve the living God. Hebrews 9:13-14

For this cause he is the mediator of the New Testament. That by means of death, for the redemption of the transgressions that were under the first testament, they who are called might receive the promise of eternal inheritance. For where a testament is, there must also of necessity be the death of the testator. The testament is of force only after men are dead. Otherwise it is of no strength at all while the testator lives. Hebrews 9:15-17

Comparing the Two Testaments

The first testament was dedicated with blood. Moses spoke every precept to all the people according to the law. Then he took the blood of calves and goats, with water, scarlet wool, and hyssop, and sprinkled both the book, and all the people. He said: This is the blood of the testament, which God has joined himself to you. Then he sprinkled the tabernacle, and all the vessels of the ministry with blood. And by the law, almost all things are purged with blood; and without the shedding of blood, there is no remission. Hebrews 9:18-22

It was necessary therefore that the earthly things, which were patterned after the heavenly, should be purified with these. But the heavenly things are purified with better sacrifices than these. For Christ did not enter into the holy places made with hands, which are the figures of the true; but into heaven itself, now to appear in the presence of God for us. Hebrews 9:23-24

Not that he should offer himself often, as the high priest entered into the holy place every year with blood for others. Then he would have suffered many times, from the foundation of the world until now. But once, at the end of the world, he has appeared to put away sin by the sacrifice of himself. Hebrews 9:25-26

As it is appointed to men to die only once, and after this comes the judgment. So Christ was offered once to bear the sins of many. Then he will appear to those who look for him a second time without sin unto salvation. Hebrews 9:27-28

What I'm trying to share with you here is that Jesus brought us the New Testament that has a more perfect tabernacle that was made without hands, and the ceremony that is performed within it makes it possible for mankind to go to heaven and stand before God. Although this tabernacle and ceremony is not specifically described in the verses above, it is possible to know about this tabernacle and its ceremony.

The New Testament Temple

We were just shown that the physical temple was patterned after the true temple; so to find the spiritual temple, we need to look at the physical temple to find our answers. The first temples were actually called tabernacles, because they were more like tents because they needed to be mobile while they were traveling in the desert. Then once the Jewish people arrived in Jerusalem, they built a permanent building, which was called the Temple. Then there was a second temple built, after the first temple was destroyed. And now that the second temple has been destroyed, the Jews are looking forward to the building of the third temple. This third temple I assume will be built just before the second coming of Jesus, since the Bible tells us that the second temple was built for the first coming of Jesus. Using this logic, the third temple will be completed for the second coming of Jesus close to the time of the end.

Although the Jewish people had multiple temples, the pattern of how they were built remained the same. It had two main rooms. The first room was called the holy of holies. Its length, width, and height were equal; making it a perfectly shaped room where the presence of God the Father resided, showing that he is Holiest of all.

The other room was the sanctuary. Its width and height were of equal dimensions, and the length of the room was twice as long as the width and height. The size of this room was like taking two perfectly shaped rooms of equal length, width, and height, and sliding them together. The reason this room is shaped like two perfect rooms slid together is that this room contains the two next holiest of all, which are the Son and the Holy Spirit. Then when you look at these two rooms together, you get the Godhead trinity of the Father, Son, and Holy Spirit.

The Holy of Holies is for God the Father

Christians know that the Holy of Holies is for God the Father. The verse below is one of many verses that explain that God resided in this room.

And the Lord said unto Moses, Speak unto Aaron thy brother, that he come not at all times into the holy place within the veil before the mercy seat, which is upon the ark; that he die not: for I will appear in the cloud upon the mercy seat. Leviticus 16:2

God is now in his throne room in heaven. This is the holy of holies of the New Testament temple.

The Veil of the Sanctuary represents Jesus, the Son of God

The Bible verses below tell us that Jesus is the veil of the true temple.

Having therefore, brethren, boldness to enter into the holiest by the blood of Jesus, by a new and living way, which he hath consecrated for us, **through the veil, that is to say, his flesh**; Hebrew 10:19-20

In the earthly temple, some of the blood of the animal sacrifices was sprinkled on the veil of the temple. This blood represented the sins of the people. So the purpose of the veil of the earthly temple was to bare the sins of the people. And as we know, Jesus came to earth as the Lamb of God, and took upon himself the sins of the people. His body bore the sins of the world, just as the veil of the physical temple once did.

The Menorah of the Sanctuary Represents the Holy Spirit

The following verses explain that the Holy Spirit is represented by the menorah in the earthly temple. The menorah is a large decorative candlestick having seven branches, and stands before God in the sanctuary of the temple. To understand how the menorah represents Holy Spirit in the true temple made without hands, we must look to the Book of Revelation 1:4-5. These verses give us greetings from the Godhead of God the Father, the Holy Spirit, and Jesus.

John to the seven churches which are in Asia: Grace be unto you, and peace, **from him which is, and which was, and which is to come** (God the Father); and from **the seven Spirits which are before his throne** (Holy Spirit); And from **Jesus Christ**, who is the faithful witness, and the first begotten of the dead, and the prince of the kings of the earth. Unto him that loved us, and washed us from our sins in his own blood, Revelation 1:4-5

In the physical temple, if you were standing before God, you would be standing in the sanctuary of the temple. The menorah stands in the sanctuary and has seven lamps on one lamp stand. The Holy Spirit is the seven holiest angels of heaven that make up the one Holy Spirit, just like how the Holy Trinity is three in one. These are the holiest angels who perform the temple services in the true temple, along with Jesus who is its High Priest.

The Altar of Incense

This altar, also known as the "golden altar" or the "inner altar", resided in the sanctuary by the veil. It had hot coals and was sprinkled with incense which offered up a sweet smell before God. On the Day of Atonement, the High Priest would sprinkle the blood that represents the people on the horns of this altar, and the smoke would rise up before God. In the heavenly temple, this altar is before the throne of God, and carries the prayers of the saints up before God, as explained below.

And another angel came and stood at the altar, having a golden censer; and there was given unto him much incense, that he should offer it with the prayers of all saints upon the golden altar which was before the throne. And the smoke of the incense, which came with the prayers of the saints, ascended up before God out of the angel's hand. Revelation 8:3-4

The Table of Showbread

This table resided in the sanctuary, opposite of the menorah. It contained twelve loaves of bread which was changed every Sabbath. The twelve loaves represented the twelve elders of Israel. In the true temple, there are 24 elders in a circle around the throne of God, which represents the twelve elders of Israel and the twelve elders (disciples) of Jesus, as found in the verse below.

And round about the throne were four and twenty seats: and upon the seats I saw four and twenty elders sitting, clothed in white raiment; and they had on their heads crowns of gold. Revelation 4:4

The Door to the Sanctuary

The door to the true temple sanctuary is the earthly temple. The true temple sits on the same spot as the physical temple. The difference is that the true temple is vertical. The door to the sanctuary is here on earth, and the temple reaches up to heaven to the throne room of God, which is the holy of holies.

The Altar of Sacrifice

The altar of sacrifice is Jerusalem.

And he said to them, Defile the house, and fill the courts with the slain, now go forth. And they went forth, and slew in the city. And it came to pass while they were slaying them that I was left, and I fell on my face, and cried, and said, Ah Lord God! Will you destroy all the residue of Israel in your pouring out of your fury upon Jerusalem? Then he said to me: The iniquity of the house of Israel and Judah is exceeding great, the land is full of blood, and the city is full of perverseness. For they say, The Lord has forsaken the earth, and the Lord does not see. But as for me, my eye will not spare, neither will I have pity, but I will recompense their way upon their head. And, behold, the man who is clothed with linen, which had the inkhorn by his side, reported the matter, saying, I have done as you have commanded me. Eze 9:7-11

The Outer Court

The Outer Court of the physical temple was a large area outside of the temple that contained the altar of sacrifice, and the door to the temple.. The outer court of the true temple is the earth, as explained below.

But the court which is without the temple leave out, and measure it not; for it is given unto the Gentiles: and **the holy city** shall they tread under foot forty and two months. Revelation 11:2

The outer court is the earth. And sitting on outer court of the physical temple was the altar of sacrifice, which is the city of Jerusalem in the true temple. The door to the sanctuary opened to the outer court of the physical temple, and the door to the true temple opens up to the physical temple in Jerusalem. What these verses above are showing is that Jerusalem is part of the outer court.

Jesus will Rule in Jerusalem

Jesus will rule in Jerusalem, because Jerusalem is part of the true temple. And he will rule after the order of Melchisedec, and not after the order of Aaron, as the verse below explains.

Whither the forerunner is for us entered, even Jesus, made a high priest forever after the order of Melchisedec. Hebrews 6:20

What is the order of Melchisedec? The Bible explains it this way.

For this Melchisedec, king of Salem, priest of the most high God, who met Abraham returning from **the slaughter of the kings**, and **blessed him**; To whom also **Abraham** gave a tenth part of all; first being by interpretation King of righteousness, and after that also King of Salem, which is, King of peace; Without father, without mother, without descent, having neither beginning of days, nor end of life; but made like unto the Son of God; abides a priest continually. Now consider how great this man was, unto whom even the patriarch Abraham **gave the tenth of the spoils**. Hebrews 7:1-4

Although these verses talk about Melchisedec, they do not tell us who he was. But one day I found this same event in the Book of Jasher. When you compare the passages below with the passages above, you discover that this High Priest was Shem, the son of Noah.

And Abram heard this, and he rose up with about three hundred and eighteen men that were with him, and he that night **pursued these kings and smote them,** and they all fell before Abram and his men, and there was none remaining but the four kings who fled, and they went each his own road. Jasher 16:7

And Adonizedek **king of Jerusalem**, the same was **Shem**, went out with his men to meet **Abram** and his people, with bread and wine, and they remained together in the valley of Melech. And **Adonizedek blessed Abram**; and Abram **gave him a tenth** from all that he had **brought from the spoil** of his enemies, for Adonizedek was **a priest before God**. Jasher 16:11-12

So when Jesus rules after the order of Melchisedec, he will be the King and the High Priest in Jerusalem, which we are taught in the Bible that he will be.

What is the Book of Jasher?

The Book of Jasher is the same book that was read by some of the Old Testament prophets, as these two prophets gave witness in the Bible.

"Is not this written in the Book of Jasher? Joshua 10:13.

"Behold it is written in the Book of Jasher." 2nd Samuel 1:18

Why Can't We See The True Tabernacle?

After Jesus rose from the dead, he ascended up into heaven and to God. So the logical question is where is heaven? Actually, heaven is not as far away as you may think, as the verses below explain:

And God made the firmament, and divided the waters which were under the firmament from the waters which were above the firmament: and it was so. **And God called the firmament Heaven**. And the evening and the morning were the second day. Genesis 1:7-8

And God said: Let the waters bring forth abundantly the moving creature that hath life, and fowl that may fly above the earth **in the open firmament of heaven**. Genesis 1:20

These verses tell us that heaven is the area between the ground and the clouds, and that the birds fly in heaven. Yet we cannot see heaven. Since God says that heaven is between the seas and the clouds, but we cannot see heaven, there can be only one explanation; heaven is invisible to mankind. I'm not saying here that heaven does not extend beyond the clouds and into outer space, but that heaven is invisible to mankind and that heaven is where these verses says it is.

THE NEW TESTAMENT CEREMONY

The Daily Sacrifice

The earthly temple was patterned after the true temple, and since there was a ceremony performed in the earthly temple, we can be sure there is a ceremony being performed in the true temple.

The earthly temple is what connected the Jewish people to God. Its main function was to remove sin from the people so that they could worship God in the Temple. There are two main ceremonies that were performed for this purpose, and they were the daily sacrifice, and the cleansing of the sanctuary, also called the Day of Atonement. We will cover the daily sacrifice ceremony first.

Basically, the daily sacrifice ceremony was the daily sacrifice of animals in the temple. The purpose of the animals was to be the substitution sacrifice for the persons who brought the animal sacrifice. First the priest would confess the sins of the people onto the animal, and then the animal was killed, and then some of the blood was sprinkled onto the veil of the temple. Once this ceremony has been completed, the person who brought the animal sacrifice was considered temporarily cleansed from sin until he sinned again.

This continued for generations, but God grew weary of the blood of the animal sacrifices. So he sent his son as the Lamb of God, to put an end to the need of daily sacrifices of animals. This is the "taking away of the daily sacrifice" that the Book of Daniel talks about.

The daily sacrifice ceremony was to be used for the sinners, but is not necessary for the sinless, meaning Jesus Christ. When Jesus lived a sinless life, the need for animal sacrifices came to an end, and now all are to be saved through the body and blood of Jesus. This is the message of the Last Supper when Jesus and his disciples partook of the ceremony of the bread and wine, which represented his blood and body that he offered up on the cross. This is also the same message of the Communion Service we now practice in our churches.

Then at the death of Jesus, the old covenant came to an end and the reason for the daily sacrifice was taken away. Then the New Testament came into effect. The veil in the temple was torn in two and God returned to his throne in heaven; because the temple ceremonies moved into the true tabernacle made without hands. And now Jesus, our High Priest, is performing the temple ceremonies in the true temple made without hands in heaven.

The Cleansing of the Sanctuary

With the need for the daily sacrifice taken away, it is time for the second part of the temple ceremony. The second part of the physical temple ceremony was the cleansing of the sanctuary ceremony, which was also called the Day of Atonement. This ceremony was performed once a year in the temple, and its purpose was to cleanse the temple, and the entire nation of Israel of sin, all at the same time. Once this ceremony was completed, the nation of Israel was considered cleansed from all sin. The problem with this Old Testament ceremony was that it was not a permanent removal of sin, and was only for the nation of Israel. The New Testament of Jesus is permanent and is for all mankind.

We can recognize the true temple Day of Atonement ceremony, because the earthly tabernacle ceremony was patterned from it. And now the Day of Atonement ceremony is being performed in the true tabernacle made without hands. This ceremony is what allows us to go into heaven, and what we will be studying next.

The Ceremony Started Here on Earth

Although the New Testament did not come into effect until the death of Jesus, it was necessary for him to begin the Day of Atonement ceremony of the true temple while he was still here on earth before his death. The beginning of this ceremony takes place on the outer court and before the door of the sanctuary, which we just discovered are here on earth.

Again we can recognize these steps of this ceremony, because we know the earthly ceremonies were patterned after the heavenly. So next we are going to compare the Day of Atonement verses of the Old Testament, found in Leviticus chapter 16, with the acts of the time of Jesus that explain where these verses are fulfilled in the New Testament. Again, the beginning of this ceremony starts here on earth and is described in the Gospels, and then it transitions into the Book of Revelation when the ceremony moves inside the true temple. Now the ceremony begins.

The Putting on of the Priestly Garments

Old Testament

This is how Aaron shall come into the holy place: with a young bullock for a sin offering and a ram for a burnt offering. He shall put on the holy linen coat, and he shall have the linen breeches upon his flesh, and shall be girded with a linen girdle, and with the linen mitre shall he be attired: these are holy garments; therefore shall he wash his flesh in water, and so put them on. Leviticus 16:3-4

New Testament

Jesus is the young bullock sin offering. The burnt offering isn't needed in the true temple ceremony, since Jesus was able to go physically before God. The Book of Revelation describes Jesus in his priestly garments, in the verses below.

And in the midst of the seven churches was the Son of man, in a garment clothed down to his feet, and tied about the breast with a golden belt. His head and his hairs were white like wool, as white as snow; his eyes looked like a flame of fire; his feet looked like fine brass burning in a furnace; and his voice sounded like the voice of a multitude. In his right hand he had the Holy Spirit which are the angels of the seven churches: out of his mouth went a sharp sword, which is the Word of God: and his body shone as bright as the sun shining in its strength. Revelation 1:13-16 paraphrased

Choosing the Two Sin Offerings from the People

Old Testament

And he shall take of the congregation of the children of Israel two kids of the goats for a sin offering, and one ram for a burnt offering. Leviticus 16:5

New Testament

The two sin offerings are: the scribes and Pharisees, and the disciples of Jesus. The burnt offering is not needed, because the disciples of Jesus will physically go to heaven once we are forever cleansed from sin, and we will stand before God on the sea of glass.

The Sin Offering for the High Priest

Old Testament

And Aaron shall offer his bullock of the sin offering, which is for himself,
Leviticus 16:6a

New Testament

As described below; Jesus, as our High Priest, offered up his life for our sins as the Lamb of God.

On the next day much people that were come to the feast, when they heard that Jesus was coming to Jerusalem, Took branches of palm trees, and went forth to meet him, and cried, Hosanna: Blessed is the King of Israel that cometh in the name of the Lord. And Jesus, when he had found a young ass, sat thereon; as it is written, Fear not, daughter of Sion: behold, thy King cometh, sitting on an ass's colt. John 12:12-15

Atonement for the Bullock Sin Offering

Old Testament

and make an atonement for himself, and for his house. Leviticus 16:6b

Atonement Definition

Atonement: to atone for ones actions, to take something that was done wrong and make it right.

New Testament

Because Jerusalem did not recognize him as the Lamb of God, the city was later destroyed by the Romans.

And when he was come near, he beheld the city, and wept over it, saying: If you had known, even you, at least in this your day, the things which belong to your peace! But now they are hid from your eyes. For the days shall come upon you, that your enemies shall cast a trench about you, and compass you round, and keep you in on every side, and shall lay you even with the ground, and your children within you; and they shall not leave in you one stone upon another; because you did not know the time of your visitation. Luke 19:41-44

Presenting the Two Sin Offerings before the Lord

Old Testament

And he shall take the two goats, and present them before the Lord at the door of the tabernacle of the congregation. Leviticus 16:7

New Testament

The temple in Jerusalem is the door to the true temple. Jesus taught daily at the temple. And he was at the temple along with his disciples, and the scribes and Pharisees.

Identifying the Two Sin Offerings of the People

Old Testament

And Aaron shall cast lots upon the two goats; one lot for the Lord, and the other lot for the scapegoat. Leviticus 16:8

New Testament

Jesus chose his 12 disciples, and warned the people against the scribes and Pharisees.

Offering the Sin Offering for the People

Old Testament

And Aaron shall bring the goat upon which the Lord's lot fell, and offer him for a sin offering. Leviticus 16:9

New Testament

Jesus sent his disciples to all nations where they would be martyred for their faith.

Atonement for the Scapegoat

Old Testament

But the goat, on which the lot fell to be the scapegoat, shall be presented alive before the Lord, to make an atonement with him, and to let him go for a scapegoat into the wilderness. Leviticus 16:10

New Testament

The scapegoat is the scribes and Pharisees, and they were alive before the Lord in Jerusalem. Below is their atonement, which Jesus gave them in Jerusalem.

Woe unto you, scribes and Pharisees, hypocrites! Because you build the tombs of the prophets, and garnish the sepulchers of the righteous, and say, if we had been in the days of our fathers, we would not have been partakers with them in the blood of the prophets. Wherefore you are witnesses unto yourselves, that you are the children of them which killed the prophets. Fill you up then the measure of your fathers. You serpents, you generation of vipers, how can you escape the damnation of hell? Wherefore, behold, I send unto you prophets, and wise men, and scribes: and some of them you shall kill and crucify; and some of them shall you scourge in your synagogues, and persecute them from city to city: That upon you may come all the righteous blood shed upon the earth, from the blood of righteous Abel unto the blood of Zacharias son of Barachias, whom you slew between the temple and the altar. Verily I say unto you, all these things shall come upon this generation. O Jerusalem, Jerusalem, thou that kill the prophets, and stone them which are sent unto thee, how often I would have gathered thy children together, even as a hen gathered her chickens under her wings, and you would not! Matthew 23:29-37

The Sin Offering for the High Priest is killed

Old Testament

And Aaron shall bring the bullock of the sin offering, which is for himself,
Leviticus 16:11a

New Testament

And Jesus, our High Priest, came as the Lamb of God and offered himself for a sin offering.

Atonement for the High Priest and his House

Old Testament

and shall make an atonement for himself, and for his house, Leviticus 16:11b

New Testament

We cannot yet go to heaven with Jesus, but once Jesus completes the ceremony, we will be with him.

Let not your heart be troubled: you believe in God, believe also in me. In my Father's house are many mansions: if it were not so, I would have told you. I go to prepare a place for you. And if I go and prepare a place for you, I will come again, and receive you unto myself; that where I am, there you may be also. And wherever I go you know, and the way you know. John 14:1-4

The Lamb of God Sin Offering is killed

Old Testament

and shall kill the bullock of the sin offering which is for himself:
Leviticus 16:11c

When Jesus therefore had received the vinegar, he said: It is finished: and he bowed his head, and gave up the ghost. John 19:30

Why Jesus was crucified without the Gate

The verses below tell us why he was crucified without the gate of the city.

We have an altar, whereof they have no right to eat which serve the tabernacle. For the bodies of those beasts, whose blood is brought into the sanctuary by the high priest for sin, are burned without the camp. Wherefore Jesus also, that he might sanctify the people with his own blood, suffered without the gate. Let us go forth therefore unto him without the camp, bearing his reproach. Hebrews 13:10-13

These verses make reference to the ritual of the red heifer ceremony. This ceremony requires a rare red heifer without spot, without blemish, and has never been yoked. It must be perfect in every way. And the purpose of this ritual is to purify those who were in contact with the dead, or to put it another way, it is a ritual that purifies the impure. What the above verses are saying is that Jesus was crucified without the camp, because he is the sacrifice that cleanses the dead; and makes those who are impure, pure again.

The Day of Atonement Ceremony Moves to the Book of Revelation

This is the point where the Day of Atonement Ceremony moves inside the true temple, and is described in the Book of Revelation, starting with chapter four. Since I want to share with you the complete Book of Revelation, we will need to take a break from the Day of Atonement study. Next we will just read the first three chapters of Revelation that have been de-mystified and paraphrased into easy reading. Then we will pick up the Day of Atonement study again, starting with chapter four.

The Book of Revelation

Chapter 1

This is the Revelation of God, which he gave to Jesus Christ. The purpose of this revelation is to show the servants of Jesus the things that must shortly come to pass. Once Jesus received this revelation from his father, he sent it to his servant and disciple John, by way of his angel. To be clear here, the progression was from God the Father, to Jesus, to the angel of Jesus, to his disciple John, who was one of the original twelve disciples. The angel of Jesus was both the messenger and the seal of authenticity, meaning that by Jesus sending his personal angel, John knew that this revelation truly came from him. Then when the angel of Jesus showed this revelation to John, John recorded the word of God, the testimony of Jesus Christ, and all the things that he saw. Blessed is he who reads and those who hear the words of this prophecy, and remember the things that are written herein: for the time is at hand. Rev 1:1-3 paraphrased

John, to the seven churches which were in Asia Minor: Grace and peace be unto you from God who is, was, and is to come; and from the Holy Spirit, who are the seven Holiest Spirits standing before his throne; and from Jesus Christ, who is the faithful witness, the first begotten of the dead, and the prince of the kings of the earth. Jesus is the one who loved us and washed us from our sins in his own blood, and has made us kings and priests unto God, his Father. To him be glory and dominion forever and ever, Amen. Behold, Jesus will come with angels; and every eye will see him, and they also which pierced him. All families of the earth shall wail because of him: Even so, Amen. I am Alpha and Omega, the beginning and the ending, says the Lord, who is, was, and is to come, the Almighty. Rev 1:4-8 paraphrased

I am John, your brother and companion in tribulation, and in the kingdom and patience of Jesus Christ. I was exiled on the island that is called Patmos, for my speaking the word of God, and for my testimony of Jesus Christ. While I was there, I was in the Spirit on the Lord's Day, when I heard behind me a great voice that sounded like a trumpet saying; I am Alpha and Omega, the first and the last. What you see, write in a book, and send it to the seven churches which are in Asia; to Ephesus, Smyrna, Per-ga-mos, Thy-a-ti-ra, Sardis, Philadelphia, and La-od-i-ce-a. And I turned to see the voice that spoke with me. And after I turned, I saw the seven churches; and in the midst of the seven churches was the Son of man, in a garment clothed down to his feet, and tied about the breast with a golden belt. His head and his hairs were white like wool, as white as snow; his eyes looked like a flame of fire; his feet looked like fine brass burning in a furnace; and his voice sounded like the voice of a multitude. In his right hand he had the Holy Spirit which are the angels of the seven churches: out of his mouth went a sharp sword, which is the Word of God: and his body shone as bright as the sun shining in its strength. And when I saw him, I fell at his feet as dead. And he laid his right hand upon me saying; Fear not, I am the first and the last: I am he who was alive and then crucified; and behold, I am alive for evermore, Amen; and I have the keys of hell and death. Write the things that you have seen, the things that are, and the things which shall be hereafter. Rev 1:9-19 paraphrased

Chapter 2

These letters to the angels of the seven churches are the letters to the Holy Spirit. The Holy Spirit is the seven angels standing before the throne of God, and they were sent to comfort the churches. The first letter is God's words to comfort the church going through the first seal, and the second letter is for the church going through the second seal, and so forth.

And to the angel of the church of Ephesus (Ephesus means: desirable) write: These things say Jesus, the one who holds the angels of the seven churches his right hand, and who walks in the midst of the seven churches. I know your works, labor, and patience; and how you cannot stand them that are evil. You have tried them, who say they are apostles, but are not, and have found them to be liars. You have continued, and have patience. For my name's sake you have labored, and not fainted. Nevertheless I am somewhat against you, because you have taken your sight off of God the Father, who was your first love. So remember from where you are fallen, and repent, and do the first works. Or else I will come to you quickly, and remove your church out of its place, except you repent. But this you have, that you hate the deeds of the Nic-o-la-i-tans, which I also hate. He that has an ear let him hear what the Holy Spirit says to the churches. I will give to him that overcomes to eat from the tree of life that is in the midst of the paradise of God. Rev 2:1-7 paraphrased

And to the angel of the church in Smyrna [means: myrrh, (bitter taste, sweet smelling)] write: These things say the first and the last, he who was dead, and is alive. I know your works, tribulation, and poverty, (but you art rich). And I know the blasphemy of them, who say they are Jews but are not, for they are the synagogue of Satan. Fear none of those things that you will suffer. Behold, the devil will cast some of you into prison that you may be tried, and you will have tribulation ten days. Be faithful unto death, and I will give you a crown of life. He who has an ear let him hear what the Holy Spirit says to the churches. He who overcomes will not be hurt of the second death. Rev 2:8-11 paraphrased

And to the angel of the church in Per-ga-mos (means: height), write: These things says Jesus who has the sharp sword with two edges. I know your works, and where you dwell, even where Satan's seat is. You hold fast my name, and have not denied my faith, even in those days when Antipas was my faithful martyr, who was slain among you, where Satan dwells. But I have a few things against you, because you have there, those who follow the doctrine of Ba-laam, who was the son of Beor the soothsayer, and was very wise and understood the art of witchcraft. He's also the one who taught King Balac how to get the children of Israel to stumble by getting t the children of Israel to eat things sacrificed to idols, and to commit fornication. You also have there, those who follow the doctrine of the Nic-o-la-i-tans, which thing I hate. Repent, or else I will come to you quickly, and fight against them with the sword of my mouth. Let those who have an ear, hear what the Holy Spirit says to the churches. I will give to those who overcome the hidden manna to eat, and a white stone. And in the stone will be written a new name, which no man knows except the one who receives it. Rev 2:12-17 paraphrased

And to the angel of the church of Thy-a-ti-ra (means: sacrifice of labor) write: These things say the Son of God, who has eyes that look like a flame of fire, and feet like fine brass. I know your works, charity, service, faith, patience, and works; and the last to be more than the first. Notwithstanding I have a few things against you, because you allow that woman Jezebel, who proclaims herself that the she is a prophetess, to teach and seduce my servants to commit fornication, and to eat things sacrificed to idols. I gave her space to repent of her fornication, but she would not. Look, I will cast her into a bed, and those who commit adultery with her, into great tribulation, except they repent of their deeds. I will kill her children with death, and all the churches will know that I am the one who searches the reins and hearts. I will give to every one of you according to your works. But to you and to the rest in Thyatira I say, as many as do not follow this doctrine, and have not known the depths of Satan, as they speak; I will put on you no other burden. But that which you have already, hold fast till I come. And to him who overcomes and keeps my works to the end, I will give power over the nations. He will rule them with a rod of iron. As the vessels of a potter will they be broken to shivers, even as I received of my Father. And I will give him the morning star. Let those who have an ear, hear what the Holy Spirit says to the churches. Rev 2:18-29 paraphrased

Chapter 3

And to the angel of the church in Sardis (means: escaping ones or those who come out) write: These things say Jesus who has the seven Spirits of God, and the angels of the seven churches. I know your works that you have a name that you live, but are dead. Be watchful, and strengthen the things that remain, that are ready to die. For I have not found your works perfect before God. So remember how you have received and heard, hold fast, and repent. But if you will not watch, I will come on you as a thief, and you will not know what hour I will come on you. You have a few names even in Sardis which have not defiled their garments, and they will walk with me in white, for they are worthy. He that overcomes, the same will be clothed in white raiment, and I will not blot out his name out of the book of life, but I will confess his name before my Father, and before his angels. Let all that has an ear, hear what the Holy Spirit says to the churches. Rev 3:1-6 paraphrased

And to the angel of the church in Philadelphia (means: brotherly love) write; These things says Jesus who is holy, he who is true, he who has the key of David, he that opens and no man shuts, and shuts and no man opens. I know your works. Look, I have set before you an open door that no man can shut. For you have a little strength, and have kept my word, and have not denied my name. Behold, I will make them of the synagogue of Satan, who say they are Jews and are not, but do lie; behold, I will make them to come and worship before your feet, and to know that I have loved you. Because you have kept the word of my patience, I will also keep you from the hour of temptation, which will come upon the entire world, to try them that live on the earth. Behold, I come quickly. Hold fast to that which you have that no man may take your crown. To him who overcomes I will make a pillar in the temple of my God, and he will not go out anymore. And I will write on him the name of my God, and the name of the city of my God, which is New Jerusalem, which will come down out of heaven from my God. And I will write on him my new name. He that has an ear let him hear what the Holy Spirit says to the churches. Rev 3:7-13 paraphrased

And to the angel of the church of the La-od-i-ce-ans (means: just people) write: These things says the Amen, the faithful and true witness, the beginning of the creation of God; I know your works, that you are neither cold nor hot: I would prefer you were cold or hot. So then because you are lukewarm, and not cold nor hot, I will spit you out of my mouth. Because you say, I am rich, and increased with goods, and have need of nothing; and you do not know that you are wretched, miserable, poor, blind, and naked. I counsel you to buy from me gold tried in the fire, that you may be rich; and white raiment, that you may be clothed, and that the shame of your nakedness does not appear; and anoint your eyes with eye salve, that you may see. As many as I love, I rebuke and chasten. Be zealous therefore, and repent. Behold, I stand at the door, and knock. If any man hears my voice, and opens the door, I will come in to him, and will drink with him, and he with me. To him that overcomes will I grant to him to sit with me in my throne, even as I also overcame, and sat down with my Father in his throne. He that has an ear let him hear what the Holy Spirit says to the churches. Rev 3:14-22 paraphrased

Now that we have reached chapter four of the Book of Revelation, we will continue with our study of the Day of Atonement Ceremony that takes place in the true tabernacle made without hands. This is the point where the ceremony transitions from earth to heaven. God was within the veil in the earthly temple, but now he is in his throne room in heaven.

The High Priest Stands before God

Old Testament

And he shall take a censer full of burning coals of fire from off the altar before the Lord, and his hands full of sweet incense beaten small, and bring it within the veil: And he shall put the incense upon the fire before the Lord, that the cloud of the incense may cover the mercy seat that is upon the testimony, that he die not: Leviticus 16:12-13

New Testament

The incense in the earthly temple was used so that the High Priest could not behold God, but this is not necessary for Jesus. This altar of incense is in heaven and is used to carry the prayers of the saints up before God. But using a cloud of incense is not necessary for Jesus, because Jesus is sinless, and you must be sinless to behold the presence of God. Although Jesus did not require the incense upon the coals of the altar, I included below another scene in heaven that mentions the censer and the golden altar showing that these items also exist in the true temple, and are used to raise the prayers of the saints up before God.

And another angel came and stood at the altar, having a golden censer; and there was given unto him much incense, that he should offer it with the prayers of all saints upon the golden altar which was before the throne. And the smoke of the incense, which came with the prayers of the saints, ascended up before God out of the angel's hand. Revelation 8:3-4

Since Jesus did not need to bring incense with him when he enters before God, the requirement is that he brings himself before the presence of God. Chapter 4 begins with the disciple John taken from the isle of Patmos up into heaven by the angel of Jesus, where he witnesses Jesus standing before the Throne of God in chapter 5

Chapter 4 - The Throne Room of God is the Holiest of All

After this I looked up, and saw a door was open in heaven. And I heard the voice of the angel of Jesus sounding like a trumpet, saying: Come up here, and I will show you the things that must come hereafter. And immediately I was in the spirit, and saw God setting on his throne in heaven. His appearance was like jasper and a sardine stone. Over the throne there was a rainbow shining like an emerald, and out of the throne came lightning, thunder, and voices. Before the throne was seven lamps of fire burning that are the seven Spirits of God, and a sea of glass that looked like crystal. Sitting in a circle around the throne were twenty-four elders sitting on their twenty-four seats, clothed in white raiment with crowns of gold on their heads. Inside this circle were four cherubim in a smaller circle around the throne, and they were full of eyes in front and behind. The first one was like a lion, the second was like a calf, the third had the face of a man, and the fourth was like a flying eagle. And the four cherubim had six wings

23

around them. And they were full of eyes within, and they did not rest day or night, saying; holy, holy, holy, Lord God Almighty, who was, is, and is to come. And when those cherubim gave glory, honor, and thanks to God, who lives forever and ever, the twenty-four elders fell down before God who was sitting on his throne, and they worship him who lives forever and ever. They cast their crowns before the throne, saying; You are worthy, O Lord, to receive glory, honor, and power; for you have created all things, and for your pleasure they are and were created. Rev 4:1-11 paraphrased

Chapter 5 - The Sacrificial Lamb Enters the Holiest of All

And John, saw that God had a book in his right hand that was sealed with seven seals, and he could see that the book had writing on the inside and on its back. Then John saw a strong angel proclaiming with a loud voice: Who is worthy to remove the seals and open the book? And no man in heaven, on earth, or under the earth, was able to open this book, or to look on it. Then I wept bitterly, because no one was found worthy to open and read the book, or to look upon it. Then one of the elders said to him, do not weep. Look, the Lion of the tribe of Judah, the Root of David, has prevailed to open the book and to remove its seven seals. So I looked, and saw Jesus, the Lamb that was slain, and he had the Holy Spirit, which is the seven Spirits of God sent forth into all the earth. Rev 5:1-6 paraphrased

And he was standing in the midst of the throne, the four cherubim, and elders; and he came and took the book out of the right hand of God who was sitting on his throne. And when he took the book, the four cherubim and the twenty-four elders fell down before Jesus, every one of them having harps and golden vials full of odors, which are the prayers of saints. And they sang a new song, saying; you are worthy to take the book, and to open its seals. For you was slain, and have redeemed us to God by your blood out of every family, tongue, people, and nation. You have made us kings and priests to our God, and we will rule on the earth. And I saw and heard the voices of many angels that were around the throne, cherubim, and elders. The number of them was one hundred and one million. And they said with a loud voice: Worthy is Jesus, the Lamb who was slain, to receive power, riches, wisdom, strength, honor, glory, and blessing. Then every creature that was in heaven, on the earth, under the earth, and all that are in the sea, heard John saying: Blessing, honor, glory, and power be to God, and to Jesus, forever and ever. And the four cherubim said:

Amen. And the twenty-four elders fell down and worshipped God who lives forever and ever. Rev 5:7-14 paraphrased

The Seven Flicks of Blood Represents the Seven Seals

In the verse below, the High Priest next flicks the blood that is for the High Priest and his family on the mercy seat seven times. Nothing else happens here. When we see the corresponding verses in the second covenant, we see that these flicks of blood represent seven major things that will be initiated from the holy of holies, which is now the throne room of God. The first four seals take place in Europe and the Middle East, and the rest are worldwide.

Old Testament

And he shall take of the blood of the bullock, and sprinkle it with his finger upon the mercy seat eastward; and before the mercy seat shall he sprinkle of the blood with his finger seven times. Leviticus 16:14

New Testament

Chapter 6

First Seal

And I saw Jesus open one of the seals, and I heard the sound of thunder. Then I heard one of the four cherubim saying, come and see. So I looked, and I saw a white horse with the Pharisees sitting as the head of the church. And the Roman Emperors used the Roman Army to help the Pharisees attack the Christians; and these Pharisees went forth conquering and to conquer. Rev 6:1-2 paraphrased

Second Seal

And when Jesus opened the second seal, I heard the second cherubim say, Come and see. And there went out War, riding on another horse that was red, and power was given to him to take peace from the earth, that

they should kill one another, and there was given to him a great sword.
Rev 6:3-4 paraphrased

Third Seal

And when Jesus opened the third seal, I heard the third cherubim say, come and see. And I looked, and saw Hunger riding on a black horse, with a pair of balances in his hand. And I heard a voice in the midst of the four cherubim say: A measure of wheat for a penny, and three measures of barley for a penny. See that you do not hurt the oil and the wine.
Rev 6:5-6 paraphrased

Fourth Seal

And when Jesus had opened the fourth seal, I heard the voice of the fourth cherubim say, "Come and see". And I looked, and saw Death riding on a pale horse, and Hell followed with him. And power was given to them over the fourth part of the earth to kill with sword, hunger, death, and with the war machines of the earth. Rev 6:7-8 paraphrased

Fifth Seal

And when Jesus opened the fifth seal, I saw in the graves, the souls of them that were slain for the word of God, and for the testimony that they held. And they cried with a loud voice, saying: How long, O Lord, holy and true, before you judge and avenge our blood on those who dwell on the earth? And white robes were given to every one of them. And it was said to them, that they should rest yet for a little season, until their fellow servants also and their brethren, that should be killed as they were, should be fulfilled. Rev 6:9-11 paraphrased

Sixth Seal

And I saw when Jesus had opened the sixth seal, and behold, there were nuclear explosions like a great earthquake. The sun turned black, as black as sackcloth of hair, because of the dust and debris in the air. And during the night the moon turned to the color of blood, because of the nuclear fallout. Rev 6:12-13 paraphrased

And you could see the flames of the rockets as they came down from the upper atmosphere. They looked like the stars of heaven falling to the earth, even as a fig tree drops her figs, when she is shaken of a mighty wind. The mushroom cloud they created looked like a scroll that was rolled together in heaven being unrolled. Every mountain and island was moved out of their places. The kings of the earth, the great men, rich men, chief captains, mighty men, every bondman, and every free man, hid themselves in the dens and rocks of the mountains. And they said to the mountains and rocks, fall on us, and hide us from the face of God who sits on the throne, and from the wrath of the Lamb. For the great day of his wrath is come, and who will be able to stand? Rev 6:14-17 paraphrased

Chapter 7

And after these things I saw four angels standing on the four corners of the earth, holding the four winds of the earth, that the wind should not blow on the earth, the sea, or on any tree. And I saw another angel ascending from the east, having the seal of the living God. And he cried with a loud voice to the four angels to whom it was given to hurt the earth and the sea, saying: Do not hurt the earth, the sea, or the trees, until we have sealed the servants of our God in their foreheads. Rev 7:1-3 paraphrased

The 144,000 is sealed

And I heard the number of them that were sealed, and there were sealed one hundred and forty-four thousand of all the tribes of the children of Israel. Twelve thousand of each tribe was sealed, of the tribe of Judah, Reuben, Gad, Aser, Nephthalim, Manasses, Simeon, Levi, Issachar, Zabulon, Joseph, and Benjamin. Rev 7:4-8 paraphrased

The High Priest's Family is taken into Heaven

After this I looked, and saw a great multitude, which no man could number, of all nations, families, people, and tongues, stood before the throne and before the Lamb, clothed with white robes and palms in their hands. And they cried with a loud voice, saying, Salvation to our God who sits upon the throne, and to the Lamb. And all the angels stood round about the throne, and about the elders and the four cherubim. And they fell before the throne on their faces, and worshipped God saying, Amen,

Blessing, glory, wisdom, thanksgiving, honor, power, and might, be to our God forever and ever, Amen. And one of the elders answered, saying to me: What are these, which are arrayed in white robes? And where did they come from? And I said to him, Sir, you know. And he said to me: These are they, which came out of great tribulation, and have washed their robes, and made them white in the blood of the Lamb. Therefore they are before the throne of God, and serve him day and night in his temple. And God, who sits on the throne, will dwell among them. They will not hunger or thirst anymore. The sun will not shine on them, or any heat. For the Lamb, which is in the midst of the throne, will feed them and lead them to living fountains of waters. And God will wipe away all tears from their eyes. Rev 7:9-17 paraphrased

Chapter 8

Seventh Seal

And when Jesus opened the seventh seal, there was silence in heaven about the space of half an hour. Rev 8:1 paraphrased

The cleansing of the High Priest and his family is complete, and all those who are saved through the body and blood of Jesus are standing before God in heaven. Now the seven seals on the scroll have been broken, and now the writings on the scroll can be fulfilled. What comes next is the second chance for those who are lukewarm, and those who just could not commit to following Jesus. But there is a price to pay for their disbelief. They will have to go through the tribulations of the seven trumpets.

The Sin Offering for the People

The sin offering for the people is the disciples, later called Christians. They offered up their lives for their faith, and shed their blood from the time of the ascension of Jesus, until this time. Jesus came to preach the gospel in Israel, and the disciples were sent out to preach the gospel to all nations. It is their acts that made it possible to save the rest of the people of the world.

After the rapture of the church, there will be no question about who is right, and who is wrong. This is the time period for those who remain to re-examine their relationship with Jesus. Those who overcome will be brought into the throne room of God at the end of this cleansing, and those who cannot change will remain.

Old Testament

Then shall he kill the goat of the sin offering that is for the people, and bring his blood within the veil, Leviticus 16:15a

New Testament

Then I saw the Holy Spirit, which are the seven angels standing before God, and they were given seven trumpets. Then Jesus came and stood at the altar, holding a golden censer. And much incense was given to him, so that he could offer it, along with the prayers of all the saints upon the golden altar, which is before the throne of God. And the smoke of the incense, along with the prayers of the saints, ascended up before God out of the hand of Jesus. And Jesus took the censer, filled it with fire from the altar, and threw it to the earth: and there were voices, thundering, lightning, and an earthquake. And the seven angels of the Holy Spirit, which had the seven trumpets, prepared themselves to sound. Rev 8:2-6 paraphrased

The Cleansing of the People

Old Testament

and do with that blood as he did with the blood of the bullock, and sprinkle it upon the mercy seat, and before the mercy seat: Leviticus 16:15b

New Testament

First Trumpet

The first angel of the Holy Spirit sounded, and there followed hail and fire mingled with blood raining down upon the earth. All the green grass and a third part of trees was burnt up. Rev 8:7 paraphrased

Second Trumpet

And the second angel sounded, and what looked like a great mountain burning with fire was thrown into the sea. A third part of the sea turned to blood; a third part of the creatures which were in the sea, and had life, died; and a third part of the ships were destroyed. Rev 8:8-9 paraphrased

Third Trumpet

And the third angel sounded, and there fell a great star from heaven, burning like a lamp, and it fell upon the third part of the rivers, and upon the fountains of waters. And the name of the star is called Wormwood, and the third part of the waters became wormwood. And many men died of the waters, because they were made bitter. Rev 8:10-11 paraphrased

Fourth Trumpet

And the fourth angel sounded, and the third part of the sun, the moon, and the stars was smitten, so that their light was dimmed by the third part. One-third of the daylight was dimmed, and the night likewise. And I saw, and heard an angel flying through the midst of heaven, saying with a loud voice, Woe, woe, woe, to those who live on the earth by reason of the other voices of the trumpet of the three angels, which are yet to sound!
Rev 8:12-13 paraphrased

Chapter 9

Fifth Trumpet

And the fifth angel sounded, and I saw Satan fall from heaven to the earth, and he was given the key of the bottomless pit. And when he opened the bottomless pit, smoke rose out of it, like the smoke of a great furnace. The smoke of the pit darkened the sun and the air, and out of the smoke came helicopters upon the earth. And these helicopters were given power, as the scorpions of the earth have power. And they were commanded to not hurt the grass of the earth, or any green thing, or any tree, but only those men who do not have the seal of God in their foreheads. They were commanded to not kill them, but to torment them five months. And their torment was as the torment of a scorpion, when he strikes a man. And in those days men will seek death, but not find it. They will desire to die, and death will flee from them. And the shapes of the helicopters were like horses prepared for battle, and their rotors looked like crowns of gold on their heads. They had faces of men, long hair like women, and microphones coming out of their helmets shaped like the teeth of lions. Their breastplates were made of iron, and when they flew they made a sound like many horses running to battle. Their tail rotors looked like scorpions tails that are rolled up, they sprayed liquid from their tails like scorpion stings, and their power was to hurt men five months. And they had a king over them, which is the angel of the bottomless pit, whose name in the Hebrew tongue is Abaddon, but in the Greek tongue is named Apollyon. These names interpreted means destroyer and this angel of the bottomless pit is Satan. He is also the king over the eighth kingdom, which is part of the seventh kingdom. One woe is past; and look, two more woes are still coming after this. Rev 9:1-12 paraphrased

Sixth Trumpet

And the sixth angel sounded, and I heard a voice from the four horns of the golden altar which is before God, Saying to the sixth angel which had the trumpet, Loose the four angels which are bound in the great river Euphrates. And the four angels were loosed, which were prepared for an hour, and a day, and a month, and a year, for to slay the third part of men. And the number of the army of tanks was two hundred million, and I heard the number of them. And thus I saw the tanks in the vision, and those who sat in them, having breastplates of fire, jacinth, and sulfur. The heads of the canons of the tanks looked like heads of lions; and out of their mouths came fire, smoke, and sulfur. By these three was the third part of men killed, by the fire, smoke, and sulfur, which came out of their mouths. For their power is in the mouth and barrel of the tanks: for their barrels looked like serpents, and had heads, and with them they do hurt. And the rest of the men which were not killed by these plagues still did not repent of the works of their hands, that they should not worship devils and idols of gold, silver, brass, stone, and wood; which cannot see, hear, or walk. And they did not repent of their murders, sorceries, fornication, or thefts. Rev 9:13-22 paraphrased

Chapter 10

And I saw another mighty angel come down from heaven, clothed with a cloud, and a rainbow was upon his head, and his face shone like the sun, and his feet looked like pillars of fire. And he had in his hand a little book open. And he set his right foot upon the sea, and his left foot on the earth, and he cried with a loud voice, as when a lion roars. And when he had cried, the seven thunders uttered their voices. And when the seven thunders had uttered their voices, I was about to write: and I heard a voice from heaven saying to me, Seal up those things which the seven thunders uttered, and do not write them. And the angel that I saw stood upon the sea and upon the earth. And he lifted up his hand to heaven and swore by God who lives forever and ever, who created heaven and all things that are in it; the earth and all things that are in it; and the sea and the things which are in it. He swore that there should be time no longer. But in the days of the voice of the seventh angel, when he shall begin to sound, the mystery of God should be finished, as he had declared to his servants the prophets. And the voice that I heard from heaven spoke to me again, and said, go and take the little book, which is open in the hand of the angel, which stands upon the sea and upon the earth. And I went to the angel, and said to him, give me the little book. And he said to me, Take it, and eat it up. It will be sweet as honey in your mouth, but it will make your belly bitter. And I took the little book out of the angel's hand, and ate it up. It was in my mouth sweet as honey, and as soon as I had eaten it, my belly was bitter. And he said to me: You must prophesy again before many peoples, nations, tongues, and kings. Rev 10:1-11 paraphrased

Chapter 11

And I was given a reed the length of a rod. And the angel stood, saying, rise, and measure the temple of God, the altar, and those who worship inside. But leave out the court, which is outside the temple, and do not measure it. For it is given to the Gentiles, and the holy city they will tread under foot forty-two months. Rev 11:1-2 paraphrased

And I will give power to my great army, the 144,000 of the tribe of Israel who were sealed: for they are my two witnesses, and they will prophesy a thousand two hundred and sixty days, clothed in sackcloth. These are the two olive trees, and the two candlesticks standing before the God of the earth. And if any man will hurt them, fire proceeds out of their mouth,

32

and devours their enemies. And if any man will hurt them, he must be killed in this manner. These have power to shut heaven that it does not rain in the days of their prophecy. And have power over waters to turn them to blood, and to smite the earth with all plagues, as often as they want. Rev 11:3-6 paraphrased

And when they have finished their testimony, the Empire that ascends out of the bottomless pit will make war against them, and shall overcome them, and kill them. And their dead bodies will lie in the street of the great city, Jerusalem, which spiritually is called Sodom and Egypt, where also our Lord was crucified. And all of the people, families, tongues, and nations will see their dead bodies three and one-half days, and will not bother to put their dead bodies in graves. And all who live on the earth will rejoice over them and make merry, and send gifts to one another; because these two prophets tormented those who live on the earth. And after three and one-half days, the Spirit of life from God entered into them, and they stood on their feet; and great fear fell upon those who saw them. And they heard a great voice from heaven saying to them, Come up here. And they ascended up to heaven in a cloud, and their enemies watched them. And the same hour there was a great earthquake, and the tenth part of the city fell, and in the earthquake were slain seven thousand men, and the remnant were afraid, and gave glory to the God of heaven. The second woe is past; and behold, the third woe comes quickly. Rev 11:7-14 paraphrased

Seventh Trumpet

And the seventh angel sounded; and there were great voices in heaven, saying: The kingdoms of this world have become the kingdoms of our Lord and of his Christ; and he will reign forever and ever. Rev 11:15 paraphrased

Atonement for the Holy Place

Old Testament

And he shall make an atonement for the holy place, because of the uncleanness of the children of Israel, and because of their transgressions in all their sins: Leviticus 16:16a

New Testament

And the twenty-four elders, which sat before God on their seats, fell on their faces, and worshipped God, Saying, We give thee thanks, O Lord God Almighty, which are, was, and are to come; because you have taken to you your great power, and have reigned. Rev 11:16-17 paraphrased

Atonement for the Tabernacle of the Congregation

Old Testament

and he shall make an atonement for the tabernacle of the congregation, that remains among them in the midst of their uncleanness. Leviticus 16:16b

New Testament

The nations were angry, and your wrath is come: and the time of the dead that they should be judged, and that you should give reward to your servants the prophets, saints, and those who fear your name, small and great; and to destroy those who destroy the earth. Rev 11:18 paraphrased

The Tabernacle is closed until the Atonement is completed

Old Testament

And there shall be no man in the tabernacle of the congregation when he goes in to make an atonement in the holy place, until he come out, and have made an atonement for himself, and for his household, and for all the congregation of Israel. Leviticus 16:17

New Testament

And the temple of God was opened in heaven, and there was seen in his temple the ark of his testament: and there were lightning, voices, thundering, an earthquake, and great hail. Rev 11:19 paraphrased

The Atonement for the Altar of Sacrifice

Old Testament

And he shall go out unto the altar that is before the Lord, and make an atonement for it; Leviticus 16:18a

New Testament

This altar is located on the other side of the sanctuary, and is called the altar of sacrifice. This altar represents the earth. The atonement for this altar is the following confessions of what Satan and his followers have done here on the earth.

Chapter 12 - Satan Crucified Jesus and Forced the Israelites out of Israel

And there appeared a great wonder in heaven. It was Israel portrayed as a woman clothed with the sun, with the moon under her feet, and upon her head a crown of twelve stars, which represent the twelve tribes of Israel. And because the woman was with child, she cried, travailing in birth and pained to be delivered. And there appeared another wonder in heaven. I saw Satan, portrayed as a great red dragon, having seven heads and ten horns, and seven crowns on his heads. The seven heads represent the seven mountains that Rome sits on. The ten horns represent the ten provinces that made up the country of Rome before its conquests toward the south, and east, and the pleasant land. The seven crowns on the seven heads shows that this kingdom was ruled from the city of Rome. When you put these together, it tells us that this happened during the time period of the Ancient Roman Empire. And the dragons' tail drew the third part of the angels of heaven, and cast them to the earth. And the dragon stood before the woman, which was ready to be delivered, to devour her child as soon as it was born. And she brought forth the man-child Jesus, who was to rule all nations with a rod of iron, and her child was caught up to God, and to his throne. Rev 12:1-5 paraphrased

And the woman fled into the wilderness, where she had a place prepared of God that they should feed her there one thousand two hundred and sixty days. Rev 12:6 paraphrased

When Satan was cast out of Heaven, he persecuted the Israelites and made war with the Christians

And there was war in heaven. Michael and his angels fought against the dragon, and the dragon fought and his angels, but they did not prevailed. Neither was there a place found for them anymore in heaven. And the great dragon was cast out, that old serpent, called the Devil, and Satan, which deceives the whole world. He was cast out into the earth, and his angels were cast out with him. Rev 12:7-9 paraphrased

And I heard a loud voice saying in heaven: Now comes salvation and strength, the kingdom of our God, and the power of his Christ. For the accuser of our brethren, which accused them before our God day and night, is cast down. And they overcame him by the blood of the Lamb and by the word of their testimony, for they did not love their lives to their death. Therefore rejoice you heavens, and you who live in them. But woe to all those who live on the earth and in the sea!: For the devil has come down to you, having great anger, because he knows that his time is short. Rev 12:10-12 paraphrased

And when Satan saw that he was cast unto the earth, he persecuted Israel, which brought forth Jesus. And a large airplane was given to Israel, so she could fly into the wilderness, into her place, where she will be nourished for three and one-half years, away from the face of Satan. And Satan sent a large number of people to go after the Israelites, to destroy them. But the people of the earth helped the Israelites, and the people of the earth sent their own people, and killed those who were sent by Satan. And Satan was angry with the Israelis, and went to make war with the Christians, who are the remnant of her seed, which keep the commandments of God, and have the testimony of Jesus Christ. Rev 12:13-17 paraphrased

Chapter 13 - Satan Raised up His World Kingdom

And I stood upon the sand of the sea, and saw the Babylon rise up out of the people. It included the city of Rome and the ten countries that made up ancient Rome before its conquests south and east and the pleasant land. The kings of the ten countries ruled the Empire, and upon the kings heads were the name of blasphemy. And Babylon, which I saw was an Empire and included the areas of the Empires of Grecia, Mede-Persia, and Ancient Babylon. And Satan gave it his power, seat, and great authority.

Although it seemed that Babylon was destroyed in the nuclear war, it's deadly wound was healed. And the entire world wondered after Babylon. And they worshipped Satan, who gave power to the Babylon Empire. And they worshipped the Babylon Empire, saying: Who can compare to Babylon? Who is able to make war with them? And there was given to him a mouth speaking great things and blasphemies; and power was given to him to continue forty-two months. And he opened his mouth in blasphemy against God, to blaspheme his name, his tabernacle, and those who live in heaven. And it was given to him to make war with the saints, and to overcome them. And power was given to him over all families, languages, and nations. And all that live on the earth will worship him, whose names are not written in the book of life of the Lamb slain from the foundation of the world. If any man has an ear, let him hear. He that leads into captivity shall go into captivity. He who kills with the sword must be killed with the sword. Here is the patience and the faith of the saints. Rev 13:1-10 paraphrased

Satan Raised up his One World Religion

And I saw the false prophet coming up out of the earth; and he had two horns like a lamb, but he spoke like Satan. And he ruled with all the power of Babylon, and causes the earth and those who live in it, to worship the Babylon Empire whose deadly wound was healed. And he did great wonders, so that he makes fire come down from heaven on the earth in the sight of men, and deceives them who live on the earth by the means of those miracles which he had power to do in the sight of the Empire: Saying to them who live on the earth, that they should make an image to Babylon, which had the wound by a sword, and did live. And he had power to give life to the image of Babylon, that the image of Babylon should both speak, and cause as many that would not worship the image of Babylon should be killed. And he caused all, the small and great, rich and poor, bond and free, to receive a mark in their right hand or in their foreheads: that no man could buy or sell, except he has the mark, or the name of Babylon, or the number of his name. Here is wisdom. Let him that has understanding count the number of Babylon: for it is the number of the false prophet; and his number is six hundred sixty, six. Rev 13:11-18 paraphrased

The Altar of Sacrifice

Chapter 14

Old Testament

and shall take of the blood of the bullock, and of the blood of the goat, and put it upon the horns of the altar round about. Leviticus 16:18b

New Testament

The altar of sacrifice is the earth. The bride of Jesus and the saints are upon the earth. The blood of Jesus and the Christians cleanse the saints who are on the earth. Therefore the bride and the saints will be taken off of the earth, but those who are not saved will be sacrificed upon the earth.

The Bride of Jesus

And I looked, and saw Jesus standing on Mount Sion, which is on the north side of Jerusalem, and with him were the one hundred and forty-four thousand, who had his Father's name written in their foreheads. And I heard God's voice from heaven, and his voice sounded like the voice of a multitude, and like the sound of great thunder. And I heard the voice of the harp players singing as they played their harps. And they sang a new song before the throne, the four cherubim, and the elders. And no man could learn that song but the one hundred and forty-four thousand, which were redeemed from the earth. These are the ones who were not defiled with women, for they are virgins. These are the ones who follow the Lamb wherever he goes. Who were redeemed from among men, and are the first fruits unto God and to the Lamb. Dishonesty was not found in their mouth, and they are without fault before the throne of God.

Rev 14:1-5 paraphrased

The Patience of the Saints

And I saw another angel fly in the midst of heaven, having the everlasting gospel to preach to every nation, family, language, and people that lives on the earth: Saying with a loud voice: Fear God, and give glory to him.

For the hour of his judgment is come. Worship him that made the heaven, earth, sea, and fountains of waters. Rev 14:6-7 paraphrased

And there followed another angel, saying: Babylon is fallen, is fallen, that great city, because she made all nations drink from the wine of the wrath of her fornication. Rev 14:8 paraphrased

And the third angel followed them, saying with a loud voice: If any man worships the beast and his image, and receives his mark in his forehead or in his hand, The same will drink of the wine of the wrath of God, which is poured out without mixture into the cup of his indignation. And he will be tormented with fire and sulfur in the presence of the holy angels, and in the presence of Jesus. And the smoke of their torment will ascend up forever and ever. And they who worship Babylon and his image, and receive the mark of his name will not have any rest day or night. Rev 14:9-11 paraphrased

Here is the patience of the saints. Here are they that keep the commandments of God, and the faith of Jesus. And I heard a voice from heaven saying to me: Write, Blessed are the dead, which die in the Lord from this point on. Yes says the Spirit, that they may rest from their labors and their works will follow them. Rev 14:12-13 paraphrased

Those Who Are Saved Are Taken To Heaven

And I looked, and I saw the Son of man sitting on a white cloud, with a golden crown on his head, and a sharp sickle in his hand. And another angel came out of the temple, crying with a loud voice to Jesus who was sitting on the cloud: Thrust in your sickle and reap, for the time is come for you to reap; for the harvest of the earth is ripe. And Jesus thrust in his sickle on the earth, and the earth was reaped. Rev 14:14-16 paraphrased

Those Who Are Not Saved Are Cast Into the Winepress of the Wrath of God

And another angel came out of the temple, which is in heaven, he also having a sharp sickle. And another angel came out from the altar, which had power over fire. And he cried with a loud cry to him that had the sharp sickle, saying: Thrust in your sharp sickle, and gather the clusters of the vine of the earth; for her grapes are fully ripe. And the angel thrust in his sickle into the earth, and gathered the vine of the earth, and cast it into the great winepress of the wrath of God. And the winepress was trodden outside the city. And blood flowed out of the winepress. The flow was as high as the horse bridles, and two hundred miles long. Rev 14:17-20 paraphrased

Chapter 15 - The Saints Are Taken to Heaven

And I saw another sign in heaven, great and marvelous, seven angels having the seven last plagues; for in them is filled up the wrath of God. And I saw what looked like a sea of glass mingled with fire: and them that had gotten the victory over the beast, and over his image, and over his mark, and over the number of his name, standing on the sea of glass, having the harps of God. And they sang the song of Moses the servant of God and the song of the Lamb, saying: Great and marvelous are your works, Lord God Almighty. Just and true are your ways. You are the King of the saints. Who will not fear you, O Lord, and glorify your name? For only you are holy. All nations will come and worship before you, for your judgments are made manifest. Revelation 15:1-4 paraphrased

The Sacrifice of Those Who Are Not Saved Begins

And after that I looked, and saw the temple of the tabernacle of the testimony in heaven was opened. And the seven angels came out of the temple, having the seven plagues. And they were clothed in pure and white linen that was tied breast high with a golden belt. And one of the four cherubim gave the seven angels the seven golden vials full of the wrath of God. Then the temple was filled with smoke from the glory and power of God. And no man was able to enter into the temple, till the seven plagues of the seven angels were fulfilled. Revelation 15:5-8 paraphrased

Chapter 16

The Cleansing of the Earth

In the verse below, the High Priest next flicks blood on the altar. Nothing else happens here. When we see the corresponding verses in the second covenant, we see that these flicks of blood represent seven things that will be initiated.

Old Testament

And he shall sprinkle of the blood upon it with his finger seven times, and cleanse it, and hallow it from the uncleanness of the children of Israel. Leviticus 16:19

New Testament

First Vial

And I heard God's voice out of the temple saying to the seven angels: Go your ways, and pour out the vials of the wrath of God on the earth. And the first angel went, and poured out his vial on the earth; and a noisome and grievous sore fell upon the men who had the mark of the beast, and on those who worshipped his image. Revelation 16:1-2 paraphrased

Second Vial

And the second angel poured out his vial upon the sea; and the sea became as the blood of a dead man. And every living soul died in the sea. Revelation 16:3 paraphrased

Third Vial

And the third angel poured out his vial on the rivers and fountains of waters, and they turned to blood. And I heard the angel of the waters say: You are righteous, O Lord, which are, was, and will be, because you have judged thus; For they have shed the blood of saints and prophets, and you have given them blood to drink; for they are worthy. And I heard another say from out of the altar, Even so, Lord God Almighty, true and righteous are your judgments. Revelation 16:4-7 paraphrased

Fourth Vial

And the fourth angel poured out his vial on the sun; and power was given to him to scorch men with fire. And men were scorched with great heat, and blasphemed the name of God, which has power over these plagues: and they did not repent and give him glory. Revelation 16:8-9 paraphrased

Fifth Vial

And the fifth angel poured out his vial on the seat of the empire; and his kingdom was full of darkness; and they gnawed their tongues for pain, and blasphemed the God of heaven because of their pains and sores, and did not repent of their deeds. Revelation 16:10-11 paraphrased

Sixth Vial

And the sixth angel poured out his vial on the great river Euphrates; and the water of the river was dried up, that the way of the kings of the east might be prepared. And I saw three unclean spirits like frogs come out of the mouth of the Satan, the image of Babylon, and the false prophet; for they are the spirits of devils, working miracles, which go forth to the kings of the earth and the whole world, to gather them to the battle of that great day of God Almighty. Behold, I come as a thief. Blessed is he that watches, and keeps his garments, lest he walks naked, and they see his shame. And he gathered them together into a place called in the Hebrew tongue Armageddon. Revelation 16:12-16 paraphrased

Seventh Vial

And the seventh angel poured out his vial into the air; and there came a great voice out of the temple of heaven, from the throne, saying: It is done. And there were voices, thunders, lightings, and a great earthquake. And the earthquake was so mighty and so great, that there hasn't been an earthquake like it since men were on the earth. And the great city was divided into three parts, and the cities of the nation's fell. And Rome, the Great Babylon, came into remembrance before God, to give to her the cup of the wine of the fierceness of his wrath. And every island fled away, and the mountains were not found. And there fell on men great hail out of heaven, every stone's weight was around of 56 pounds. And men cursed God because of the plague of the hail; for the plague of hail was exceeding great. Revelation 16:17-21 paraphrased

The Identity of the Scapegoat

Old Testament

And when he hath made an end of reconciling the holy place, and the tabernacle of the congregation, and the altar, he shall bring the live goat: and Aaron shall lay both his hands upon the head of the live goat, and confess over him all the iniquities of the children of Israel, and all their transgressions in all their sins, putting them upon the head of the goat, and shall send him away by the hand of a fit man into the wilderness: and the goat shall bear upon him all their iniquities unto a land not inhabited: and he shall let go the goat in the wilderness. Leviticus 16:20-22

New Testament

Chapter 17

And there came one of the seven angels of the Holy Spirit, and talked with me, saying; Come here, I will show to you the judgment of the great whore who rules over many peoples, multitudes, nations, and tongues. With whom the kings of the earth will joined themselves to. And the inhabitants of the earth will be made drunk with the blood that they shed. Rev 17:1-2 paraphrased

So he carried me away in the spirit into the wilderness: and I saw a woman sit upon a scarlet colored beast, full of names of blasphemy, having seven heads and ten horns. And the woman was arrayed in purple and scarlet color, decked with gold and precious stones and pearls, and having a golden cup in her hand full of abominations and filthiness of her fornication. And upon her forehead was the name written, MYSTERY, BABYLON THE GREAT; THE MOTHER OF HARLOTS AND ABOMINATIONS OF THE EARTH. And I saw the woman drunk with the blood of the saints and with the blood of the martyrs of Jesus. And when I saw her, I wondered with great admiration. Rev 17:3-6 paraphrased

And the angel said to me: Why did you marvel? I will tell you the mystery of the woman, and the beast that carried her, which has the seven heads and ten horns. The beast that you saw was the Western Roman Empire, and then it was not an empire, and it will ascend again out of the bottomless pit, and continue until it goes into perdition. And they that live on the earth shall wonder, those whose names were not written in the book of life from the foundation of the world, when they see this Western Roman Empire that was, and is not, and yet is. Rev 17:7-8 paraphrased

And here is the mind that has wisdom. The seven heads are the seven mountains, on which Rome sits, which are called the Seven Hills of Rome. And there are seven kingdoms: the first five kingdoms that have fallen are Babylon, Mede-Persia, Grecia, Assyria, and Egypt; as described in the Book of Daniel. The one that existed during the writing of the Book of Revelation was the sixth kingdom of the Ancient Roman Empire. And the other kingdom that had not yet come was the Western Roman Empire. When this kingdom came, it continued for a short space. This is the empire that was, and was not, and yet is, it even the eighth kingdom, and is of the seventh kingdom, and goes into the Lake of Fire. This last kingdom is the kingdom that had the deadly wound by the sword, but still lived. Rev 17:9-11 paraphrased

And the ten horns that you saw are ten countries that have not received a kingdom as yet; but will receive power as king's one hour with the Empire. These have one mind, and will give their power and strength to this eighth kingdom. These will make war with Jesus, and Jesus will overcome them: for he is Lord of lords, and King of kings: and they that are with him are called, chosen, and faithful. Rev 17:12-15 paraphrased

And the ten countries that you saw on the empire will hate the city of Rome, and make her desolate and naked, and will eat her flesh, and burn her with fire. For God has put in their hearts to fulfill his will, and agree to give their kingdom to the Empire, until the words of God are fulfilled. And the woman that you saw is Rome, the great city that reigned over the kings of the earth when the Apostle John was writing the Book of Revelation. Rev 17:16-18 paraphrased

Chapter 18 - The Scapegoat is slain

And after these things I saw another angel come down from heaven, having great power; and the earth was lightened with his glory. And he cried mightily with a strong voice, saying, Babylon the great has fallen. It has fallen and become the habitation of devils, and a dwelling place of every foul spirit, and a cage for every unclean and hateful bird. For all nations have drunk of the blood she shed in anger, after she joined herself together with this eighth kingdom. And the kings of the earth have also joined themselves together with this eighth kingdom with her, and their merchants of the earth have grown rich through the abundance of her delicacies. Rev 18:1-3 paraphrased

And I heard another voice from heaven, saying: Come out of her my people, so that you are not partakers of her sins, and that you do not receive of her plagues: For her sins have reached unto heaven and God has remembered her iniquities. Rev 18:4 paraphrased

Reward her even as she rewarded you, and double unto her double according to her works. In the cup, which she has filled, fill to her double. How much she has glorified herself and lived deliciously, so much torment and sorrow give her. For she says in her heart, I sit a queen, and I am no widow, and will not see any sorrow. Therefore her plagues will come in one day, death, mourning, and famine; and she will be utterly burned with fire. For strong is the Lord God who judges her. Rev 18:5-8 paraphrased

And the kings of the earth, who joined themselves to the eighth kingdom with her, and lived deliciously with her, will mourn and lament for her, when they see the smoke of her burning. Standing far off for the fear of her torment, saying: Alas, alas, that great city Babylon, that mighty city! For in one hour your judgment has come. Rev 18:9-10 paraphrased

And the merchants of the earth will weep and mourn over her. For no man buys her merchandise anymore. The merchandise of gold, silver, precious stones, pearls, fine linen, purple, silk, and scarlet; all thyine wood, all vessels of ivory and precious wood, brass, iron, marble, cinnamon, odors, ointments, frankincense, wine, oil, fine flour, wheat, beasts, sheep, horses, chariots, slaves, and souls of men. And the fruits that your soul lusted after are departed from you, and all things that were dainty and goodly are departed from you, and you will not find them anymore at all. Rev 18:11-14 paraphrased

The merchants of these things, which were made rich by her, will stand far off for the fear of her torment, weeping and wailing, and saying: Alas, alas, that great city, that was clothed in fine linen, purple, and scarlet, decked with gold, precious stones, and pearls! For in one hour your great riches have come to nothing. Every shipmaster, and all the company in ships, and sailors, and as many as trade by sea, stood far off, and cried when they saw the smoke of her burning, saying: What city can compare to this great city! And they threw dust on their heads, and cried, weeping and wailing, saying: Alas, alas, that great city, from where all were made rich that had ships in the sea by reason of her costliness! For in one hour she is made desolate. Rev 18:14-19 paraphrased

Rejoice over her, you in heaven, and you holy apostles and prophets. For God has avenged you on her. And a mighty angel took up a stone like a great millstone, and threw it into the sea, saying: Like this, with violence, that great city Babylon will be thrown down, and will not be found anymore at all. And the voice of the harpers, musicians, pipers, and trumpeters, will not be heard anymore at all in you. And no craftsman, of whatever craft he does, will be found anymore in you. And the sound of a millstone will not be heard anymore at all in you. And the light of a candle will not shine anymore at all in you. And the voice of the bridegroom and the bride will not be heard anymore at all in you. For your merchants were the great men of the earth. For by your sorceries all nations were deceived. And in her was found the blood of the prophets, and the saints, and all that were slain on the earth. Rev 18:20-24 paraphrased

Chapter 19 – God has Judged Babylon the Great

And after these things I heard a great voice of many people in heaven, saying: Alleluia; Salvation, glory, honor, and power, unto the Lord our God. For true and righteous are his judgments: For he has judged the great whore, who corrupted the earth with her union with the eighth kingdom, and has avenged the blood of his servants at her hand. And again they said Alleluia. And her smoke rose up forever and ever. Rev 19:1-3 paraphrased

Marriage Supper of the Lamb

And the twenty-four elders and the four cherubim fell down and worshipped God, who was sitting on the throne, saying Amen, Alleluia. And a voice came out of the throne, saying: Praise our God, all you his servants, and you that fear him, both small and great. And I heard what sounded like the voice of a great multitude, and like the voice of many waters, and as the voice of mighty thundering saying, Alleluia, for the Lord God omnipotent reigns. Let us be glad and rejoice, and give honor to him: For the marriage of the Lamb has come and his wife has finished her preparation. And it was granted to her that she should be arrayed in fine linen, clean and white.

For the fine linen is the righteousness of saints. And he said to me: Write, Blessed are those who are called to the marriage supper of the Lamb. And he said to me: These are the true sayings of God. And I fell at his feet to worship him and he said to me: See that you do not do it for I am your fellow servant, and part of your brethren who have the testimony of Jesus. Worship God. For the testimony of Jesus is the spirit of prophecy. Rev 19:4-10 paraphrased

The High Priest puts on his Own Garments

Old Testament

And Aaron shall come into the tabernacle of the congregation, and shall put off the linen garments, which he put on when he went into the holy place, and shall leave them there: And he shall wash his flesh with water in the holy place, and put on his garments, Leviticus 16:23-24a

New Testament

These verses show Jesus already in his own clothes.

And I saw heaven opened, and in heaven I saw a white horse; and Jesus who sat on him was called: Faithful and True, and in righteousness he does judge and make war. His eyes were as a flame of fire, and on his head were many crowns. And he had a name written, that was known only to him. The vesture that he was wearing was dipped in blood, and his name is called The Word of God. And the armies, which were in heaven, followed him upon white horses, clothed in fine linen, white and clean. And out of his mouth goes a sharp sword, that with it he should smite the nations. And he will rule them with a rod of iron: and he did tread the winepress of the fierceness and wrath of Almighty God. And he had on his vesture and on his thigh a name written: KING OF KINGS, AND LORD OF LORDS. Rev 19:11-16 paraphrased

The Atonement of the Burnt Offerings

Old Testament

and come forth, and offer his burnt offering, and the burnt offering of the people, and make an atonement for himself, and for the people. Leviticus 16:24b

New Testament

And I saw an angel standing in the sun. And he cried with a loud voice, saying to all the fowls that fly in the midst of heaven; Come and gather yourselves together to the supper of the great God. That you may eat the flesh of kings, captains, mighty men, horses and those who sit on them, and the flesh of all men, both free and bond, small and great. Rev 19:17-19

And I saw an angel standing in the sun; and he cried with a loud voice, saying to all the fowls that fly in the midst of heaven, Come and gather yourselves together unto the supper of the great God; That ye may eat the flesh of kings, and the flesh of captains, and the flesh of mighty men, and the flesh of horses, and of them that sit on them, and the flesh of all men, both free and bond, both small and great. Rev 19:17-17 paraphrased

The Sin Offerings are burned

Old Testament

And the fat of the sin offering shall he burn upon the altar. Leviticus 16:25

New Testament

And I saw the eighth kingdom, and the kings of the earth with their armies, gathered together to make war against Jesus who that sat on the horse, and against his army. And the eighth kingdom was taken, along with the false prophet who worked miracles before the image, which he used to deceive those who had received the mark of the beast, and those who worshipped his image. These both were cast alive into a lake of fire burning with sulfur. And the remnant was slain by Jesus who sat upon the horse with the sword that came out of his mouth. And all the fowls were filled with their flesh. Rev 19:20-21 paraphrased

Chapter 20

And I saw an angel come down from heaven with the key of the bottomless pit and a great chain in his hand. And he laid hold on the dragon, that old serpent, which is the Devil, and Satan, and bound him a thousand years. And the angel threw him into the bottomless pit, and shut him up. Then he put a seal on him, that he should not deceive the nations anymore, until the thousand years have passed. And after that he must be released for a short time. And I saw thrones and the ones who sat on them, and judgment was given to them. And I saw the souls of the saints who were beheaded for the witness of Jesus and for the word of God, and the ones who did not worship the false prophet or his image, or receive his mark on their foreheads, or in their hands. And they lived and reigned with Christ for a thousand years. But the rest of the dead did not live again until the thousand years were finished. This is the first resurrection. Blessed and holy is he that has part in the first resurrection. On such the second death has no power, but they will be priests of God and Christ, and will rule with him a thousand years. Rev 20:1-6 paraphrased

And when the thousand years have expired, Satan will be released from his prison. And he will go out to deceive the nations which are in the four quarters of the earth, Gog and Magog, to gather them together to battle. The number of them will be as the sand of the sea. Rev 20:7 8 paraphrased

And they went up covering the earth, and surrounding the camp of the saints and the beloved city. And fire came down from God out of heaven, and devoured them. And the devil that deceived them was cast into the lake of fire and sulfur, where the image of the eighth kingdom and the false prophet are, and they will be tormented day and night forever and ever. And there was not found any place for them. And I saw a great white throne, and God who sat on it, from whose face the earth and the heaven fled away. Rev 20:9-11 paraphrased

And they went up covering the earth, and surrounding the camp of the saints and the beloved city. And fire came down from God out of heaven, and devoured them. And the devil that deceived them was cast into the lake of fire and sulfur, where the image of the eighth kingdom and the false prophet are, and they will be tormented day and night forever and ever. And there was not found any place for them. And I saw a great white throne, and God who sat on it, from whose face the earth and the heaven fled away. Rev 20:9-11 paraphrased

A New Heaven and a New Earth

Chapter 21

And I saw a new heaven and a new earth. For the first heaven and the first earth were passed away, and there was no more sea. And I John saw the holy city, New Jerusalem, coming down from God out of heaven, prepared as a bride adorned for her husband. And I heard a great voice out of heaven saying, Behold, the tabernacle of God is with men, and he will dwell with them, and they will be his people, and God himself will be with them, and be their God. And God shall wipe away all tears from their eyes; and there will not be any more death, sorrow, crying, or pain. For the former things are passed away. Rev 21:1-4 paraphrased

And while sitting on the throne, God said, Behold, I make all things new. And he said to me, Write: for these words are true and faithful. And he said to me: It is done. I am Alpha and Omega, the beginning and the end. I will give the fountain of the water of life freely to him who is thirsty. He who overcomes will inherit all things; and I will be his God, and he will be my son. But the fearful, unbelieving, abominable, murderers, whoremongers, sorcerers, idolaters, and all liars, will have their part in the lake that burns with fire and sulfur. This is the second death. Rev 21:5-8 paraphrased

And there came to me one of the seven angels which had the seven vials full of the seven last plagues, and talked with me, saying, Come here, I will show you the bride, the Lamb's wife. And he carried me away in the spirit to a great and high mountain, and showed me that great city, the holy Jerusalem, descending out of heaven from God, Having the glory of God. And her light looked like a most precious stone, even like a jasper stone, clear as crystal. And it had a great and high wall with twelve gates, and at the gates twelve angels, and names were written on the twelve gates, which are the names of the twelve tribes of the children of Israel: On the east three gates; on the north three gates; on the south three gates; and on the west three gates. And the wall of the city had twelve foundations, and in them the names of the twelve apostles of the Lamb. Rev 21:9-14 paraphrased

And he that talked with me had a golden reed to measure the city, the gates, and its wall. And the foundation of city was square. The length was as long as the width. And he measured the city with the reed, and it measures twelve thousand furlongs (1500 miles). The length, width, and height of it are equal. And he measured the wall, and it measured a hundred and forty-four cubits (216 feet), according to the measure of a man, that is, of the angel. And the wall was made of jasper. And the city was pure gold that looked like clear glass. And the foundations of the wall of the city were garnished with all manner of precious stones. The first foundation was jasper; the second, sapphire; the third, a chalcedony; the fourth, an emerald; The fifth, sardonyx; the sixth, sardius; the seventh, chrysolyte; the eighth, beryl; the ninth, a topaz; the tenth, a chrysoprasus; the eleventh, a jacinth; the twelfth, an amethyst. And the twelve gates were twelve pearls; every several gate was of one pearl. And the street of the city was pure gold that was transparent like glass. Rev 21:15-21 paraphrased

And I did not see a temple there: Because the Lord God Almighty and the Lamb are the temple of it. And the city did not have a need for the sun or the moon to shine in it. For the glory of God shined on it, and the Lamb is the light of it. And the nations of them which are saved will walk in its light. And the kings of the earth bring their glory and honor to it. And its gates will not be shut at all by day, and there will not be any night there. And the glory and honor of the nations they will bring into it. And there will not be anything that defiles, works abomination, or makes a lie entering into it, but only those who are written in the Lamb's book of life. Rev 21:22-27 paraphrased

Chapter 22

And he showed me a pure river of water of life, clear as crystal, proceeding out of the throne of God and of the Lamb. In the midst of its stream, and on either side of the river, there was the tree of life, which produced the twelve different fruits, and it yielded her fruit every month. And the leaves of the tree were for the healing of the nations. And the curse will be over: for the throne of God and the throne of the Lamb will be in it and his servants will serve him. They will see his face, and his name will be in their foreheads. There will not be any night there, and they will not need a candle or the light of the sun. For the Lord God gives them light, and they will reign forever and ever. And he said unto me, These sayings are faithful and true: and the Lord God of the holy prophets sent his angel to show unto his servants the things which must shortly be done. Behold, I come quickly: blessed is he that keeps the sayings of the prophecy of this book. Rev 22:1-7 paraphrased

And I John saw these things, and heard them. And when I had heard and seen, I fell down to worship before the feet of the angel which showed me these things. Then he said to me, See you do not do it. For I am your fellow servant, and of your brethren the prophets, and part of those who keep the sayings of this book. Worship God. He that is unjust, let him be unjust still. He who is filthy, let him be filthy still. He who is righteous, let him be righteous still. And he who is holy, let him be holy still. Rev 22:8-11 paraphrased

And, behold, I come quickly; and my reward is with me, to give to every man according to his work. I am Alpha and Omega, the beginning and the end, the first and the last. Blessed are those who obey the commandments. That they may have the right to the tree of life, and may enter in through the gates into the city: for without are dogs, sorcerers, whoremongers, murderers, idolaters, and those who love to make a lie. Rev 22:12-15 paraphrased

I Jesus have sent mine angel to testify unto you these things in the churches. I am the root and the offspring of David, and the bright and morning star. And the Spirit and the bride say, Come. And let him that hears say, Come. And let him that is thirsty come. And whoever will, let him partake of the water of life freely. He who testifies these things says: Surely I come quickly. Amen. Even so, come, Lord Jesus. The grace of our Lord Jesus Christ be with you all. Amen. Rev 22:16-21 paraphrased

PART 2
THE END OF THE WORLD TIMELINE

Whom shall he teach knowledge? And whom shall he make to understand doctrine? Them who are weaned from the milk, and drawn from the breasts? For precept must be upon precept, precept upon precept; line upon line, line upon line; here a little, and there a little: For with stammering lips and another tongue will he speak to this people. Isaiah 28:9-11

This is how the Bible teaches us the time of the end, a little here and a little there, but this is not what you will find here. This writing is a collection of end-time scriptures arranged into a biblical timeline of events, built around the Book of Revelation. Its purpose is to give the reader the clearest understanding possible of what will take place during the end of time as we know it. What follows is what the bible tells us will take place during the end of time. We will start at the time period leading up to the first Day of the Lord.

The Day of the Lord is coming

And after this gospel of the kingdom is published and preached in the entire world for a witness to all nations, the end will come. And when you see Jerusalem compassed with armies, know that its desolation is near. And when you see the abomination of desolation, spoken of by Daniel the prophet, stand in the holy place, (let all who read this understand), let those who are in Judah flee to the mountains. Also, let those who are in the midst of it depart out, and do not let those who are in the countries enter in. Do not let those who are on the housetop come down to take anything out of his house, nor let him that is in the field return back to take his clothes: for these are the days of vengeance that all things, which are written, may be fulfilled. Mt 24:14, Lu 21:20, Mt 24:15, Lu 21:21 (Mt 24:16), Mt 24 17-18, Mt 24:17

But there will be great sorrow for those who are with child, and for those who are nursing, in those days! For there will be great distress in the land, and vengeance upon this people. And they will fall by the edge of the sword, and be led away captive into all nations. Jerusalem will be trodden down of the Gentiles, until the times of the Gentiles is fulfilled, and pray that your flight is not in the winter, or on the Sabbath day. For then there will be great tribulation (affliction), such as was not since the beginning of the world to this time, no, nor ever shall be. And except the Lord had shortened those days, no flesh should be saved: but for the elect's sake, which he has chosen, he has shortened those days. Lu 21:23-24, Mt 24:20-21, Mr 13:20 (Mt 24:22)

But of the times and the seasons, brethren, you have no need that I write to you. For yourselves know perfectly well that the day of the Lord comes as a thief in the night. For when they shall say, Peace and safety, then sudden destruction comes upon them, as travail upon a woman with child, and they will not escape. But you brethren are not in darkness, that this day should overtake you as a thief. You are all the children of light, and the children of the day. We are not of the night, nor of darkness. Therefore let us not sleep as others do, but let us watch and be sober. For they that sleep, sleep in the night, and they that are drunk are drunk in the night. But let us, who are of the day, be sober, putting on the breastplate of faith and love; and for a helmet, the hope of salvation. For God has not appointed us to wrath, but to obtain salvation by our Lord Jesus Christ. Jesus died for us, so that whether we are awake or sleep, we will live together with him. Wherefore comfort yourselves together, and edify one another, even as you also do. 1Th 5:1-11

Now we urge you, brethren, by the coming of our Lord Jesus Christ and our gathering together to him, to not be soon shaken in mind. Nor let yourselves be troubled by spirit, word, or letter that the day of Christ is at hand. Let no man deceive you by any means. For that day will come only after the falling away, which must come first, to reveal the man of sin, who is also the son of perdition. He who opposes and exalts himself above all that is called God or that is worshipped. So that he, as God, sits in the temple of God, showing himself that he is God. Do you not remember that when I was yet with you, I told you these things? And now you know what Jesus is waiting for that he might be revealed in his time. For the mystery of iniquity does already work. Only those who now let will let, until Jesus takes them out of the way; and then that wicked one, the false prophet, will be revealed whom the Lord will consume with the spirit of his mouth, and destroy with the brightness of his coming. Even him, whose coming is after the working of Satan with all power and signs and lying wonders, deceiving through unrighteousness those who perish, because they received not the love of the truth, that they might be saved. And for this cause God will send them strong delusion, that they should believe a lie, and that all might be damned who do not believed the truth, but have pleasure in unrighteousness. 2Th 2:1-12

The Earth will be Burned

The Lord is not slack concerning his promise, as some men count slackness; but he is longsuffering toward us, not willing that any should perish, but that all should come to repentance. But the day of the Lord will come as a thief in the night, in which the heavens shall pass away with a great noise, and the elements will melt with fervent heat. The earth also and the works that are in it will be burned up. Seeing then that all these things shall be dissolved, what manner of persons ought you to be in all holy conversation and godliness. Looking for and hastening to the coming of the day of God, wherein the heavens being on fire will be dissolved, and the elements will melt with fervent heat? 2Pe 3:9-12

And I will show wonders in heaven above and signs in the earth beneath, blood, fire, and vapor of smoke. The sun will be turned into darkness and the moon into blood, before the great and terrible day of the Lord come. And it will come to pass, that whoever will call on the name of the Lord will be delivered. For in mount Zion and in Jerusalem shall be deliverance, as the Lord has said, and in the remnant whom the Lord will call. Joe 2:30-32

Now if any man builds upon this foundation gold, silver, precious stones, wood, hay, or stubble; every man's work will be made manifest. For the day will declare it, because it will be revealed by fire; and the fire will try every man's work of what sort it is. If any man's work abides which he has built upon, he will receive a reward. If any man's work is burned, he will suffer loss. But he himself will be saved, yet so as by fire. Don't you know that you are the temple of God, and that the Spirit of God dwells inside you? If any man defiles the temple of God, that man God will destroy; for the temple of God is holy, which temple you are. 1Co 3:12-17

Howl, for the day of the Lord is at hand. It will come as the destruction from the Almighty. Therefore all hands will be faint, and every man's heart will melt. They will be afraid, pangs and sorrows will take hold of them. They will be in pain as a woman during childbirth. They will be amazed one at another. Their faces will be as flames. Behold, the day of the Lord comes, cruel with both wrath and fierce anger, to lay the land desolate.

He will destroy the sinners thereof out of it. For the stars of heaven and its constellations will not give their light. The sun will be darkened in its going forth, and the moon will not cause her light to shine. I will punish the world for their evil, and the wicked for their iniquity, and I will cause the arrogance of the proud to cease, and will lay low the haughtiness of the terrible. I will make a man, more precious than fine gold or a golden wedge of Ophir. Therefore I will shake the heavens, and the earth will remove out of her place, in the wrath of the Lord of hosts, and in the day of his fierce anger. Is 13:6--13

Go now, you rich men, weep and howl for your miseries that will come on you. Your riches are corrupted, and your garments are moth-eaten. Your gold and silver is tarnished. The rust of them will be a witness against you, and will eat your flesh as if it were fire. You have heaped treasure together for the last days. Behold the hire of the laborers who have reaped down your fields, which is of you kept back by fraud, cries. And the cries of them that have reaped are entered into the ears of the Lord of Sabbath. You have lived in pleasure on the earth, and been wanton. You have nourished your hearts, as in a day of slaughter. You have condemned and killed the just, and he does not resist you. Therefore be patient brethren, unto the coming of the Lord. Behold, the husbandman waits for the precious fruit of the earth, and has long patience for it, until he receive the early and latter rain. Also be patient and establish your hearts, for the coming of the Lord draws near. Grudge not one against another, brethren, lest you are condemned. Look, the judge stands before the door. Jas 5:1-9

The Sixth Seal

Nuclear War

Enter into the rock, and hide yourselves in the dust, for fear of the Lord, and for the glory of his majesty. The lofty looks of man will be humbled, and the haughtiness of men will be bowed down, and the Lord alone will be exalted in that day: for the day of the Lord of hosts will bring low every one that is proud and lofty, and those who are lifted up. And he will bring low all the cedars of Lebanon that are high and lifted up, all the oaks of Ba-shan, all the high mountains, and all the hills that are lifted up. And also every high tower, every fenced wall, all the ships of Tar-shish, and all pleasant pictures. The loftiness of man will be bowed down, and the haughtiness of men will be made low. The Lord alone will be exalted in that day, and the idols he shall utterly abolish. They will go into the holes of the rocks, and into the caves of the earth, for fear of the Lord, and for the glory of his majesty, when he rises up to shake terribly the earth. In that day a man will cast his idols of silver and gold, which they made each one for him to worship, to the moles and to the bats. So they could go into the clefts of the rocks, and into the tops of the ragged rocks, for fear of the Lord, and for the glory of his majesty, when he rises up to shake terribly the earth. Is 2:10-21

When the Pharisees demanded of Jesus that he tell them when the kingdom of God is coming, he answered them. He told them the kingdom of God does not come with observation. They will not say, look here! Or, look there! For, behold, the kingdom of God is within you. If any man says to you, Look, here is Christ, or there, do not believe it: for false Christ's and false prophets will rise, and show signs and wonders, wanting to seduce all, and if it were possible, even the elect. But take heed, and remember that I have foretold to you all these things. Therefore if they say to you, look, he is in the desert, do not go there. Look, he is in the secret chambers, do not believe it. And he said to the disciples: The days are coming, when you will desire to see one of the days of the Son of man, and you will not see it. And they will say to you; See here, or see there. Do not go after them, or follow them. For as the lightning comes out of the east and shines even to the west so will also the coming of the Son of man be. For where ever the carcass is, there the eagles will be gathered together. Lu 17:20-21, Mt 24:23, Mr 13:22 (Mt 24:24), Mr 13:23 (Mt 24:25), Mt 24:26, Lu 17:22-23, Mt 24:27-28

And I saw when Jesus had opened the sixth seal, and behold, there were nuclear explosions like a great earthquake. The sun turned black, as black as sackcloth of hair, because of the dust and debris in the atmosphere. And the moon turned the color of blood, because of the nuclear fallout. When the rockets came, you could see the flames of the rockets as they came down from the upper atmosphere. When they came down from high up in the atmosphere, they looked like the stars of heaven falling to the earth, even as a fig tree drops her figs, when she is shaken of a mighty wind. Then when they hit the ground, the mushroom cloud they created had a top that looked like a scroll that is rolled together. Every mountain and island was moved out of their places; and the kings of the earth, the great men, rich men, chief captains, mighty men, every bondman, and every free man, hid themselves in the dens and rocks of the mountains. And they said to the mountains and rocks, fall on us, and hide us from the face of God who sits on the throne, and from the wrath of the Lamb. For the great day of his wrath is come, and who will be able to stand? Rev 6:12-17 paraphrased

The First Watch for the Return of Jesus

And in those days, immediately after that tribulation, the sun will be darkened, and the moon will not give her light. And the stars of heaven will fall, and the powers that are in heaven will be shaken. There will be signs in the sun, moon, and stars. And on the earth will be distress of nations, with perplexity, the sea and the waves roaring: men's hearts failing them for fear and for looking ahead to those things which are coming on the earth. For the powers of heaven will be shaken. And when these things begin to come to pass, then look up. Lift up your heads, for your redemption draws near. And then the sign of the Son of man will appear in heaven and all the tribes of the earth will mourn, when they see the Son of man coming in the clouds of heaven with power and great glory. And he will send his angels with a great sound of a trumpet, and they will gather together his elect from the four winds, from one end of heaven to the other. Mr 13:24 (Mt 24:29), Lu 21:25-26 & 28, Mt 24:30-31

The Parables of Jesus Coming

And he spoke to them this parable; Behold the fig tree, and all the trees. Now when they shoot forth, you see and know that summer is now nigh at hand. So likewise you, when you see these things come to pass, you know that the kingdom of God is nigh at hand, even at the doors. Verily I say to you: This generation will not pass away, until all is fulfilled. Heaven and earth will pass away, but my words will not pass away. Lu 21:29-30 (Mt 24:32), Lu 21:31 (Mt 24:33), Lu 21:32 (Mt 24:34), Mt 24:35

No man knows when that day and that hour will come, not even the angels that are in heaven, or the Son, but only the Father. You take heed, watch and pray. For you do not know when the time will come. Mr 3:32-33 (Mt 24:36)

But as the days of Noah were, so will also the coming of the Son of man be. For as in the days that were before the flood they were eating and drinking, marrying and giving in marriage, until the day that Noah entered into the ark. And they did not know until the flood came and took them all away, so shall also the coming of the Son of man be. Mt 24:37-39

Likewise also, as it was in the days of Lot. They ate, drank, bought and sold, planted, and built, but the same day that Lot went out of Sodom it rained fire and brimstone from heaven, and destroyed them all. It will even be like this in the day when the Son of man is revealed. In that day, he which is upon the housetop and his stuff in the house, do not let him come down to take it away. And he that is in the field let him likewise not return back. Remember Lot's wife. Whoever will seek to save his life will lose it, and whoever will lose his life will preserve it. Lu 17:28-33

I tell you, in that night there will be two men in one bed, one will be taken, and the other will be left. There will be two in the field, one will be taken and the other left. Two women will be grinding at the mill, one will be taken and the other left. And they answered and said to him, Where, Lord? And he said to them: Wherever the body is, there the eagles will be gathered together. Lu 17:34, Mt 24:40-41, Lu 17:37

Parables to Watch

And take heed to yourselves, unless at any time your hearts are overcharged with surfeiting, and drunkenness, and cares of this life, so that the day comes upon you unaware. For as a snare it will come on all them that live on the face of the whole earth. So watch, and pray always, that you may be accounted worthy to escape all these things that will come to pass, and to stand before the Son of man. Lu 21:34-36

You take heed, watch and pray. For you do not know when the time is. For the Son of man is as a man taking a far journey, which left his house, and gave authority to his servants, and to every man his work, and commanded the porter to watch. So you watch: for you do not know when the master of the house comes, at even, at midnight, or at the cock crowing, or in the morning: Lest coming suddenly he finds you sleeping. And what I say to you I say to all, watch. Mr 13:33-37

So watch, for you do not know what hour your Lord does come. But know this that if the good man of the house had known in what watch the thief would come, he would have watched, and would not have suffered his house to be broken up. So also be ready, for in such an hour as you do not think, the Son of man will come. Who then is a faithful and wise servant, whom his lord has made ruler over his household, to give them meat in due season? Blessed is that servant whom his lord, when he comes, will find so doing. Verily I say to you, that he will make him ruler over all his goods. But, if that evil servant says in his heart: My lord delays his coming. And if he begins to strike his fellow servants, and to eat and drink with the drunken: The lord of that servant will come in a day when he does not look for him, and in an hour that he is not aware of. And he will cut him asunder, and appoint him his portion with the hypocrites. There will be weeping and gnashing of teeth. Mt 24:42-51

The Two Witnesses

And I was given a reed the length of a rod. And the angel stood, saying, rise, and measure the temple of God, the altar, and those who worship inside. But leave out the court, which is outside the temple, and do not measure it. For it is given to the Gentiles, and the holy city they will tread under foot forty-two months. Rev 11:1-2 paraphrased

And I will give power to my two witnesses, and they will prophesy a thousand two hundred and sixty days, clothed in sackcloth. These are the two olive trees, and the two churches standing before the God of the earth. And if any man will hurt them, fire proceeds out of their mouth, and devours their enemies. And if any man will hurt them, in this manner he must be killed. These have power to shut heaven that it does not rain in the days of their prophecy. And have power over waters to turn them to blood, and to smite the earth with all plagues, as often as they want. Rev 11:3-6 paraphrased

Then I answered, and said to him: What are these two olive trees on the right side of the Holy Spirit and on the left side of it? And I answered again, and said to him: What are these two olive branches which empty the golden oil out of themselves through the two golden pipes? And he answered me and said, do you not know who these are? And I said, no, my lord. Then said he: These are the two anointed ones, who stand by the Lord of the whole earth. Zec 4:11-14 paraphrased

The Two Witnesses are Sealed

And after these things I saw four angels standing on the four corners of the earth, holding the four winds of the earth, that the wind should not blow on the earth, the sea, or on any tree. And I saw another angel ascending from the east, having the seal of the living God. And he cried with a loud voice to the four angels to whom it was given to hurt the earth and the sea, saying: Do not hurt the earth, the sea, or the trees, until we have sealed the servants of our God in their foreheads. Rev 7:1-3 paraphrased

And I heard the number of them that were sealed, and there were sealed one hundred and forty-four thousand, of all the tribes of the children of Israel. There was sealed twelve thousand of each tribe were sealed; of the tribe of Judah, Reuben, Gad, Aser, Nephthalim, Manasses, Simeon, Levi, Issachar, Zabulon, Joseph, and Benjamin. Rev 7:4-8 paraphrased

Saints Go to Heaven

And the angel of the church in Philadelphia (brotherly love) said; These things says Jesus who is holy, he who is true, he who has the key of David, he that opens and no man shuts, and shuts and no man opens. I know your works. Look, I have set before you an open door that no man can shut. For you have a little strength, and have kept my word, and have not denied my name. Behold, I will make them of the synagogue of Satan, who say they are Jews and are not, but do lie; behold, I will make them to come and worship before your feet, and to know that I have loved you. Because you have kept the word of my patience, I will also keep you from the hour of temptation, which will come upon the entire world, to try them that live on the earth. Behold, I come quickly. Hold fast to that which you have that no man may take your crown. To him who overcomes I will make a pillar in the temple of my God, and he will not go out anymore. And I will write on him the name of my God, and the name of the city of my God, which is New Jerusalem, which will come down out of heaven from my God. And I will write on him my new name. He that has an ear let him hear what the Spirit says to the churches. Rev 3:7-13 paraphrased

Come, my people, enter into your chambers, and shut your doors behind you. Hide yourself for what will seem like a little moment, until the indignation passes over. For, behold, the Lord comes out of his place to punish the inhabitants of the earth for their iniquity. The earth also will disclose her blood, and no more cover her slain. Is 26:20-21

After this I looked, and saw a great multitude, which no man could number, of all nations, families, people, and tongues, stood before the throne and before the Lamb, clothed with white robes and palms in their hands. And they cried with a loud voice, saying, Salvation to our God who sits upon the throne, and to the Lamb. And all the angels stood round about the throne, and about the elders and the four cherubim. And they fell before the throne on their faces, and worshipped God saying, Amen, Blessing, glory, wisdom, thanksgiving, honor, power, and might, be to our God forever and ever, Amen. And one of the elders answered, saying to me: What are these, which are arrayed in white robes? And where did they come from? And I said to him, Sir, you know. And he said to me: These are they, which came out of great tribulation, and have washed their robes, and made them white in the blood of the Lamb. Therefore they are before the throne of God, and serve him day and night in his temple. And God, who sits on the throne, will dwell among them. They will not hunger or thirst anymore. The sun will not shine on them, or any heat. For the Lamb, which is in the midst of the throne, will feed them and lead them to living fountains of waters. And God will wipe away all tears from their eyes. Rev 7:9-17 paraphrased

The Seventh Seal

And when Jesus opened the seventh seal, there was silence in heaven about the space of half an hour. Rev 8:1 paraphrased

And the angel of the church of the La-od-i-ce-ans (just people) says; These things says the Amen, the faithful and true witness, the beginning of the creation of God; I know thy works, that you are neither cold or hot: I would prefer you were cold or hot. So then because you are lukewarm, and not cold nor hot, I will spit you out of my mouth. Because you say, I am rich, and increased with goods, and have need of nothing; and you do not know that you are wretched, miserable, poor, blind, and naked. I counsel you to buy from me gold tried in the fire, that you may be rich; and white raiment, that you may be clothed, and that the shame of your nakedness does not appear; and anoint your eyes with eye salve, that you may see. As many as I love, I rebuke and chasten. Be zealous therefore, and repent. Behold, I stand at the door, and knock. If any man hears my voice, and opens the door, I will come in to him, and will drink with him, and he with me. To him that overcomes will I grant to him to sit with me in my throne, even as I also overcame, and sat down with my Father in his throne. He that has an ear, let him hear what the Spirit says to the churches. Rev 3:14-22 paraphrased

The Five Unwise Virgins

Then the kingdom of heaven will be like ten virgins, which took their lamps, and went out to meet the bridegroom. Five of them were wise, and five were foolish. They that were foolish did not take oil with them for their lamps, but the wise did. And while the bridegroom tarried, they all slumbered and slept. Then at midnight a cry was made, Behold, the bridegroom comes, you go out to meet him. Then all those virgins rose up, and trimmed their lamps. And the foolish said to the wise, give us some of your oil, for our lamps have gone out. But the wise answered, saying: We can't, for there might not be enough for you and us. But rather, you go to them that sell, and buy for yourselves. And while they went to buy, the bridegroom came. And they that were ready went in with him to the marriage, and the door was shut. Afterward the other virgins came also, saying, Lord, Lord, open to us, but he answered and said, Verily I say unto you, I do not know you. Watch therefore, for you do not know the day or the hour when the Son of man comes. Mt 25:1-13

Warning to the Lukewarm Servants

For the kingdom of heaven is like a man traveling into a far country: who called his own servants, and delivered to them his goods. He gave five talents to one servant, two to another, and one to another. He gave to every man, according to his unique ability, and then left on his journey. Then the one who received five talents went and traded with the talents, and made five more talents. Likewise, he that had received two talents also gained another two. But he who received one talent went and dug into the earth, and hid his lord's money. After a long time the lord of those servants came, and reckoned with them. And so the one who had received five talents came and brought another five talents, saying, Lord, you delivered to me five talents. Look, I have made you five more talents. His lord said to him: Well done, you good and faithful servant: you have been faithful over a few things, I will make you ruler over many things. Enter you into the joy of thy lord. He also who had received two talents came and said, Lord, you delivered to me two talents. Look, I have gained two more talents beside them. His lord said to him: Well done good and faithful servant. You have been faithful over a few things, and I will make you ruler over many things. Enter you into the joy of thy lord. Then he that had received the one talent came and said, Lord, I knew that you are a hard man, reaping where you have not sown, and gathering from where you have not slept. And I was afraid, and went and hid your talent in the earth. Look, there you have that is yours. His lord answered and said to him, you wicked and lazy servant, you knew that I reap where I do not sow, and gather where I have not slept. Therefore, you should have taken my money to the exchangers, so that at my coming I would have received my money with interest. Therefore, take the talent from him, and give it to the one who has ten talents. To everyone that has increase, more will be given, and he will have abundance. But from him that does not have increase; he will take away even that which he has. And he will cast you, the unprofitable servant, into outer darkness. There will be weeping and gnashing of teeth. Mt 25:14-30

The Time of the Seven Trumpets

This is the second chance for those who did not accept the grace of Jesus. When the rapture of the saints takes place, all will know that Jesus is truly the Lamb of God. This is the time when the lukewarm for Jesus will decide if they want to accept or reject Jesus. This time period will be harsh, and there will be punishments for their lack of faith.

One-Third of the Earth will be Destroy a Second Time

What comes next is the destruction of one-third of the earth. This isn't the first time this has happened though. God destroyed one-third of the earth before. It is recorded in the Book of Jasher. For those who do not recognize this book, it is the book that was read by at least two of the ancient prophets. It is mentioned twice in the Holy Bible as the verses below indicate:

And the sun stood still, and the moon stayed, until the people had avenged themselves upon their enemies. **Is not this written in the book of Jasher?** So the sun stood still, in the midst of heaven, and hasted not to go down about a whole day. Joshua 10:13

(Also he bade them teach the children of Judah the use of the bow: behold, **it is written in the book of Jasher.**) 2Samuel 1:18

If this book is good enough for the prophets Joshua and Samuel, then I feel it is good enough to use in this study. These verses below describes that

God destroyed the third part of the earth, before he totally destroyed the earth in the flood with Noah.

It was in the days of Enoch that the sons of men continued to rebel and transgress against God, and to increase the anger of the Lord against the sons of men. The sons of men went and served other gods, and they forgot the Lord who had created them in the earth. In those days the sons of men made images of brass, iron, wood, and stone, and they bowed down and served them. Every man made his god and they bowed down to them, and the sons of men turned their backs on the Lord all the days of Enoch and his children. And the anger of the Lord grew, on account of their works and abominations, which they did in the earth. And the Lord caused the waters of the river Gihon to overwhelm them. He destroyed and consumed them, and he destroyed the third part of the earth. Notwithstanding this, the sons of men did not turn from their evil ways, and their hands were yet extended to do evil in the sight of the Lord. Book of Jasher 2:3-6

The Cleansing of the Congregation Begins

Then I saw the Holy Spirit, which are the seven angels standing before God, and they were given seven trumpets. And Jesus came and stood at the altar, holding a golden censer. And much incense was given to him, so that he could offer it, along with the prayers of all the saints upon the golden altar, which is before the throne of God. And the smoke of the incense, along with the prayers of the saints, ascended up before God out of the hand of Jesus. And Jesus took the censer, filled it with fire from the altar, and threw it into the earth: and there were voices, thundering, lightning, and an earthquake. And the seven angels of the Holy Spirit, which had the seven trumpets, prepared themselves to sound. Rev 8:2-6 paraphrased

The First Trumpet

Debris from Nuclear War Falls

The first angel of the Holy Spirit sounded, and there followed hail and fire mingled with blood raining down upon the earth. All the green grass and a third part of trees was burnt up. Rev 8:7 paraphrased

The Second Trumpet

One-Third Creatures in the Sea Die

And the second angel sounded, and what looked like a great mountain burning with fire was thrown into the sea. A third part of the sea turned to blood; a third part of the creatures which were in the sea, and had life, died; and a third part of the ships were destroyed. Rev 8:8-9 paraphrased

The Third Trumpet

Wormwood Star

And the third angel sounded, and there fell a great star from heaven, burning like a lamp, and it fell upon the third part of the rivers, and upon the fountains of waters. And the name of the star is called Wormwood, and the third part of the waters became wormwood. And many men died of the waters, because they were made bitter. Rev 8:10-11 paraphrased

Therefore the Lord of hosts, the God of Israel says this; Behold, I will feed them, even this people, with wormwood, and give them water of gall to drink. Jer. 9:15

The Fourth Trumpet

Dust Cloud in the Sky

And the fourth angel sounded, and the third part of the sun, a third part of the moon, and a third part of the stars was smitten, so that their light was dimmed by the third part. Because of all the debris in the atmosphere, one-third of the daylight was dimmed, and the night likewise. And I saw, and heard an angel flying through the midst of heaven, saying with a loud voice, Woe, woe, woe, to those who live on the earth by reason of the other voices of the trumpet of the three angels, which are yet to sound! Rev 8:12-13 paraphrased

The Time of Babylon as the Eighth Empire

Satan and His Angels Are Released

God has reserved the angels, which did not keep their first estate but left their own habitation, in everlasting chains under darkness unto the great day the judgment. Jude 1:6

And there was war in heaven. Michael and his angels fought against the dragon, and the dragon fought and his angels, but they did not prevailed. Neither was there a place found for them anymore in heaven. And the great dragon was cast out, that old serpent, called the Devil, and Satan, which deceives the whole world. He was cast out into the earth, and his angels were cast out with him. Rev 12:7-9 paraphrased

The Fifth Trumpet - The First Woe

And the fifth angel sounded, and I saw Satan fall from heaven to the earth, Rev 9:1a paraphrased

And I heard a loud voice saying in heaven: Now comes salvation and strength, the kingdom of our God, and the power of his Christ. For the accuser of our brethren, which accused them before our God day and night, is cast down. And they overcame him by the blood of the Lamb and by the word of their testimony, for they did not love their lives to their death. Therefore rejoice you heavens, and you who live in them. But woe to all those who live on the earth and in the sea! For the devil has come down to you, having great anger, because he knows that his time is short. Rev 12:10-12 paraphrased

Hell from beneath is moved for you, to meet you at your coming. It stirs up the dead for you, even all the chief ones of the earth. All the kings of the nations will rise up from their thrones. All of them will speak and say to you: Have you become as weak as we are? Have you become like us? Your pomp and the noise of your viols are brought down to the grave. The worm is spread under you, and the worms cover you. How have you fallen from heaven, O Lucifer, son of the morning! How were you cut down to the ground, you who weaken the nations! For you have said in your heart, I will ascend into heaven. I will exalt my throne above the stars of God. I will also sit upon the mount of the congregation, in the sides of the north.

I will ascend above the heights of the clouds. I will be like the most High. Yet you will be brought down to hell, to the sides of the pit. They that see you will look narrowly upon you, and consider you, saying: Is this the man that made the earth to tremble, that shook kingdoms. That made the world as a wilderness, and destroyed its cities. That did not open the house of his prisoners? Is 14:9-17

And he was given the key of the bottomless pit. And when he opened the bottomless pit, smoke rose out of it, like the smoke of a great furnace. The smoke of the pit darkened the sun and the air, and out of the smoke came helicopters upon the earth. And these helicopters were given power, as the scorpions of the earth have power. And they were commanded to not hurt the grass of the earth, or any green thing, or any tree, but only those men who do not have the seal of God in their foreheads. They were commanded to not kill them, but to torment them five months. And their torment was as the torment of a scorpion, when he strikes a man. And in those days men will seek death, but not find it. They will desire to die, and death will flee from them. And the shapes of the helicopters were like horses prepared for battle, and their rotors looked like crowns of gold on their heads. They had faces of men, long hair like women, and microphones coming out of their helmets shaped like the teeth of lions. Their breastplates were made of iron, and when they flew they made a sound like many horses running to battle. Their tail rotors looked like scorpions tails that are rolled up, they sprayed liquid from their tails like scorpion stings, and their power was to hurt men five months. And they had a king over them, which is the angel of the bottomless pit, whose name in the Hebrew tongue is Abaddon, but in the Greek tongue is named Apollyon. These names interpreted means destroyer and this angel of the bottomless pit is Satan. He is also the king over the eighth kingdom, which is of the seventh kingdom. Rev 9:1b-11 paraphrased

And when Satan saw that he was cast unto the earth, he persecuted Israel, which brought forth Jesus. And a large airplane was given to Israel, so she could fly into the wilderness, into her place, where she will be nourished for three and one-half years, away from the face of Satan. And Satan sent a multitude of people after the Israelites, to destroy them. But the people of the earth helped the Israelites, and the people of the earth sent their own people, and destroyed those who were sent by Satan. And Satan was angry with the Israelites, and went to make war with the Christians, who are the remnant of her seed, which keep the commandments of God, and have the testimony of Jesus Christ. Rev 12:13-17 paraphrased

The Rise of Babylon

Satan Raises the Eighth Kingdom

And I stood upon the sand of the sea, and saw the eighth kingdom rise up out of the people. It was the seventh kingdom and the ten countries that made up ancient Rome before its conquests south and east and the pleasant land. The kings of the ten countries ruled this kingdom, and upon the kings heads were the name of blasphemy. And the eighth kingdom, which I saw was like a leopard, and his feet were as the feed of a bear, and his mouth as the mouth of a lion: and Satan gave it his power, seat, and great authority. Although it seemed that the Western Roman Empire was destroyed, but it's deadly wound was healed. And the entire world wondered after the eighth kingdom. And they worshipped Satan, who gave power to this eighth kingdom. And they worshipped the kingdom, saying: Who can compare to this kingdom? Who is able to make war with them?

The Mouth of the Eighth Kingdom

And there was given to it a mouth speaking great things and blasphemies; and power was given to him to continue forty-two months. And he opened his mouth in blasphemy against God, to blaspheme his name, his tabernacle, and those who live in heaven. And it was given to him to make war with the saints, and to overcome them. And power was given to him over all families, languages, and nations. And all that live on the earth will worship him, whose names are not written in the book of life of the Lamb slain from the foundation of the world. If any man has an ear, let him hear. He that leads into captivity shall go into captivity. He who kills with the sword must be killed with the sword. Here is the patience and the faith of the saints. Rev 13:1-10 paraphrased

Satan Establishes the False Prophet

And I saw the false prophet coming up out of the earth; and he had two horns like a lamb, but he spoke like Satan. And he ruled with all the power of the kingdom, and causes the earth and those who live in it, to worship the eighth kingdom whose deadly wound was healed. And he did great wonders, so that he makes fire come down from heaven on the earth in the sight of men, and deceives them who live on the earth by the means of those miracles which he had power to do in the sight of Satan: Saying to them who live on the earth, that they should make an image to this eighth kingdom, which had the wound by a sword, and did live.

The Church of the False Prophet

And he had power to give life to the image of the kingdom, that the image of the kingdom should both speak, and cause as many that would not worship the image of kingdom should be killed. And he caused all, the small and great, rich and poor, bond and free, to receive a mark in their right hand or in their foreheads: that no man could buy or sell, except he has the mark, or the name of kingdom, or the number of his name. Here is wisdom. Let him that has understanding count the number of the false prophet: for it is the number of a man; and his number is six hundred sixty, six. Rev 13:11-18 paraphrased

The Sixth Trumpet-The Second Woe

War with China

One woe is past; and look, two more woes are still coming after this. Rev 9:1-12 paraphrased

And the sixth angel sounded, and I heard a voice from the four horns of the golden altar which is before God, Saying to the sixth angel which had the trumpet, Loose the four angels which are bound in the great river Euphrates. And the four angels were loosed, which were prepared for an hour, and a day, and a month, and a year, for to slay the third part of men. And the number of the army of tanks was two hundred million, and I heard the number of them. Rev 9:13-16 paraphrased

And this is what I saw concerning the tanks in the vision, and those who sat in them. They had breastplates of fire, jacinth, and sulfur. The heads of the canons of the tanks looked like the heads of lions; and out of the mouths of their cannons came fire, smoke, and sulfur. And by these three was the third part of men killed, by the fire, smoke, and sulfur, which came out of their mouths. For their power is in the mouth and barrel of the tanks: for their barrels looked like serpents, and had heads, and with them they do hurt. And the rest of the men which were not killed by these plagues still did not repent of the works of their hands, that they should not worship devils and idols of gold, silver, brass, stone, and wood; which cannot see, hear, or walk. And they did not repent of their murders, sorceries, fornication, or thefts. Rev 9:17-22 paraphrased

The Little Book - Sin

And I saw another mighty angel come down from heaven, clothed with a cloud, and a rainbow was upon his head, and his face shone like the sun, and his feet looked like pillars of fire. And he had in his hand a little book open. And he set his right foot upon the sea, and his left foot on the earth, and he cried with a loud voice, as when a lion roars. And when he had cried, the seven thunders uttered their voices. And when the seven thunders had uttered their voices, I was about to write: and I heard a voice from heaven saying to me, Seal up those things which the seven thunders uttered, and do not write them. Rev 10:1-4 paraphrased

And the angel that I saw stood upon the sea and upon the earth. And he lifted up his hand to heaven and swore by God who lives forever and ever, who created heaven and all things that are in it; the earth and all things that are in it; and the sea and the things which are in it. He swore that there should be time no longer. But in the days of the voice of the seventh angel, when he shall begin to sound, the mystery of God should be finished, as he had declared to his servants the prophets. Rev 10:5-7 paraphrased

And the voice that I heard from heaven spoke to me again, and said, go and take the little book, which is open in the hand of the angel, which stands upon the sea and upon the earth. And I went to the angel, and said to him, give me the little book. And he said to me, Take it, and eat it up. It will be sweet as honey in your mouth, but it will make your belly bitter. And I took the little book out of the angel's hand, and ate it up. It was in my mouth sweet as honey, and as soon as I had eaten it, my belly was bitter. And he said to me: You must prophesy again before many peoples, nations, tongues, and kings. Rev 10:8-11 paraphrased

The Death of the Two Witnesses

And when the two witnesses have finished their testimony, the Eighth Empire that ascended out of the bottomless pit will make war against them, and shall overcome them, and kill them. And their dead bodies will lie in the street of the great city, Jerusalem, which spiritually is called Sodom and Egypt, where also our Lord was crucified. And all of the people, families, tongues, and nations will see their dead bodies three and one-half days, and will not bother to put their dead bodies in graves. And all who live on the earth will rejoice over them and make merry, and send gifts to one another; because these two prophets tormented those who live on the earth. And after three and one-half days, the Spirit of life from God entered into them, and they stood on their feet; and great fear fell upon those who saw them. And they heard a great voice from heaven saying to them, Come up here. And they ascended up to heaven in a cloud, and their enemies watched them. Rev 11:7-12 paraphrased

Jesus Returns with the 144,000

And the same hour there was a great earthquake, and the tenth part of the city fell, and in the earthquake were slain seven thousand men, and the remnant were afraid, and gave glory to the God of heaven. Rev 11:13 paraphrased

Remember when Jesus finished talking to his disciples and while they were watching, Jesus was taken up, and a cloud received him out of their sight. And while they looked intently toward heaven as he went up, behold, two men stood by them in white apparel, which also said: You men of Galilee, why do you stand gazing up into heaven? This same Jesus, who is taken up from you into heaven, will come back in like manner as you have seen him go into heaven. Ac 1:9-11 paraphrased

And his feet will stand in that day upon the Mount of Olives, which is before Jerusalem on the east, and the Mount of Olives will split in the middle of it, toward the east and toward the west, and there will be a very great valley. Half of the mountain will remove toward the north, and half of it toward the south. And you will flee into the valley of the mountains, for the valley of the mountains will reach unto Azal. Yes, you will flee, like when you fled from before the earthquake in the days of Uzziah king

of Judah. And the Lord my God will come, and all the saints with him.
Zec 14:4-5

God cried also in mine ears with a loud voice, saying: Cause them that have charge over the city to draw near, even every man with his destroying weapon in his hand. And, behold, six men came from the way of the higher gate, which lies toward the north, and every man had a slaughter weapon in his hand. One man among them was clothed with linen, with a writer's inkhorn by his side. And they went in, and stood beside the brazen altar.
Eze 9:1-2

And the glory of the God of Israel was gone up from the cherub, whereupon he was, to the threshold of the house. And he called to Jesus who was clothed with linen, and had the writer's inkhorn by his side. The Lord said to him, go through the midst of the city, through the midst of Jerusalem, and set a mark upon the foreheads of the men that sigh and that cry for all the abominations that are done in the midst of it. And to the others he said in mine hearing, you go after him throughout the city, and smite. Do not let your eye spare neither have you pity. Slay utterly old and young, both maids and little children, and women. But do not come near any man who has the mark, and begin at my sanctuary. Then they began at the ancient men, which were before the house. Eze 9:3-6

And he said to them, Defile the house, and fill the courts with the slain, now go forth. And they went forth, and slew in the city. And it came to pass while they were slaying them that I was left, and I fell on my face, and cried, and said, Ah Lord God! Will you destroy all the residue of Israel in your pouring out of your fury upon Jerusalem? Then he said to me: The iniquity of the house of Israel and Judah is exceeding great, the land is full of blood, and the city is full of perverseness. For they say, The Lord has forsaken the earth, and the Lord does not see. But as for me, my eye will not spare, neither will I have pity, but I will recompense their way upon their head. And, behold, the man who is clothed with linen, which had the inkhorn by his side, reported the matter, saying, I have done as you have commanded me. Eze 9:7-11

For when I looked, I saw a transparent deep blue throne appear in the firmament above the head of the cherubim's. And God spoke to Jesus who was clothed with linen, saying, go in between the wheels and under the cherub's, and fill your hand with coals of fire from between the cherubim's, and scatter them over the city. Then I saw them go to the temple in Jerusalem, and the cherub's stood on the right side of the house when Jesus went in, and a cloud filled the inner court. Eze 10:1-3

Then the glory of the Lord moved from the cherub's, and stood over the entrance of the house. And the house was filled with the cloud, and the court was full of the brightness of the Lord's glory. Then the sound of the cherubim's' wings was heard even to the outer court. It sounded like the voice of the Almighty God when he speaks. Eze 10:4-5

Then Jesus did as God commanded him when he said, take fire from between the wheels and cherubim's. Jesus went in and stood beside the wheels. And there appeared in the cherubim's the form of a man's hand under their wings. Then one of the cherubs stretched forth his hand into the fire that was between the cherubim's, and took coal from it. He then put it in the hands of Jesus, who took it and went out. Eze 10:6-7

And when I looked, I saw four sea-green colored wheels by the cherubim's. There was one wheel by each cherub. All four wheels looked the same and had a wheel inside of the wheel. When one wheel moved they all moved, but the wheels did not turn. Wherever the front of the wheels looked they went, and they did not turn as they moved. And their whole body; backs, hands, wings, and wheels were full of eyes all over; even the four wheels had them. As for the wheels, it was cried unto them in my hearing, O wheel. And every wheel had four faces. The first face was the face of a cherub, the second had the face of a man, the third had the face of a lion, and the fourth had the face of an eagle. Eze 10:8-14

And the cherubim's were lifted up. This is the same living creature that I saw by the river of Chebar. And when the cherubim's moved, the wheels moved with them: and when the cherubim's lifted up their wings to fly up from the earth, the same wheels that were beside them did not turn. When the cherubim stood, the wheels stood. When the cherubim went up, the wheels went up with them. For the spirit of the living creature was in them. Then the glory of the Lord left from off the threshold of the house, and stood over the cherubim's. And the cherub's lifted up their wings, and flew up from the earth in my sight. When they went out, the wheels also were beside them, and every one stood at the door of the east gate of the Lord's house; and the glory of the God of Israel was over above them. Eze 10:15-19

The second woe is past; and behold, the third woe comes quickly.
Rev 11:14 paraphrased

The Seventh Trumpet–The Third Woe

And the seventh angel sounded; and there were great voices in heaven, saying: The kingdoms of this world have become the kingdoms of our Lord and of his Christ; and he will reign forever and ever. And the twenty-four elders, which sat before God on their seats, fell on their faces, and worshipped God, Saying, We give thee thanks, O Lord God Almighty, which are, was, and are to come; because you have taken to you your great power, and have reigned. The nations were angry, and your wrath is come: and the time of the dead that they should be judged, and that you should give reward to your servants the prophets, saints, and those who fear your name, small and great; and to destroy those who destroy the earth. And the temple of God was opened in heaven, and there was seen in his temple the ark of his testament: and there were lightning, voices, thundering, an earthquake, and great hail. Rev 11:15-19 paraphrased

The Bride of Jesus

And I looked, and saw Jesus standing on Mount Sion, which is on the north side of Jerusalem, and with him were the one hundred and forty-four thousand, who had his Father's name written in their foreheads. And I heard God's voice from heaven, and his voice sounded like the voice of a multitude, and like the sound of great thunder. And I heard the voice of the harp players singing as they played their harps. And they sang a new song before the throne, the four cherubim, and the elders. And no man could learn that song but the one hundred and forty-four thousand, which were redeemed from the earth. These are the ones who were not defiled with women, for they are virgins. These are the ones who follow the Lamb wherever he goes. Who were redeemed from among men, and are the first fruits unto God and to the Lamb. Dishonesty was not found in their mouth, and they are without fault before the throne of God. Rev 14:1-5 paraphrased

The Patience of the Saints

And I saw another angel fly in the midst of heaven, having the everlasting gospel to preach to every nation, family, language, and people that lives on the earth: Saying with a loud voice: Fear God, and give glory to him. For the hour of his judgment is come. Worship him that made the heaven, earth, sea, and fountains of waters. Rev 14:6-7 paraphrased

And there followed another angel, saying: Babylon is fallen, is fallen, that great city, because she made all nations drink from the wine of the wrath of her fornication. Rev 14:8 paraphrased

And the third angel followed them, saying with a loud voice: If any man worships the beast and his image, and receives his mark in his forehead or in his hand, The same will drink of the wine of the wrath of God, which is poured out without mixture into the cup of his indignation. And he will be tormented with fire and sulfur in the presence of the holy angels, and in the presence of Jesus. And the smoke of their torment will ascend up forever and ever. And they who worship Babylon and his image, and receive the mark of his name will not have any rest day or night. Rev 14:9-11 paraphrased

Here is the patience of the saints. Here are they that keep the commandments of God, and the faith of Jesus. And I heard a voice from heaven saying to me: Write, Blessed are the dead, which die in the Lord from now on. Yes says the Spirit, that they may rest from their labors and their works will follow them. Rev 14:12-13 paraphrased

The Second Watch For Jesus

Be dressed and ready, and your lights burning. Let yourselves be like men who are waiting for their lord, waiting for him to return from his wedding. That when he comes and knocks, you may immediately open unto him. Blessed are those servants, whom the lord finds watching for him, when he comes. Verily I say to you, that he will tighten his belt about himself, and make them to sit down to eat, and will come forth and serve them. Blessed are those servants that Jesus finds ready, when he comes in both the second and third watches. And know this, that if the good man of the house had known what hour the thief was coming, he would have watched, and not allowed his house to be broken into. Therefore be ready also: For the Son of man will come at an hour when you do not expect him. Lu 12:35-40

And the Lord said: Who then is that faithful and wise steward, whom his lord will make ruler over his household, to give them their portion of meat in due season? Blessed is that servant, whom his lord finds so doing, when he comes. Of a truth I say to you, that he will make him ruler over all that he has. But and if that servant says in his heart, My lord delays his coming; and begins to beat the menservants and maidens, and eats and drinks to the point of being drunk. The lord of that servant will come in a day when he is not looking for him, and at an hour when he is not aware, and will cut him in sunder, and appoint him his portion with the unbelievers. Lu 12:42-46

And that servant, who knew his lord's will, but did not prepared himself, neither did according to his will, will be beaten with many stripes. But he that did not know, and committed things worthy of stripes, will be beaten with few stripes. For to whoever much is given, much will be required of him: and to whom men have committed much, of him they will ask the more. I have come to send fire on the earth; but what will I do, if it is already on fire? But I have a baptism to be baptized with, and I have made times difficult until it is accomplished! You suppose that I am come to give peace on earth? I tell you, No; but rather division. For from now on there will be five in one house, divided three against two, and two against three. The father will be divided against the son, and the son against the father; the mother against the daughter, and the daughter against the mother; the mother in law against her daughter in law, and the daughter in law against her mother in law. Lu 12:47-53

Those Who Are Saved Are Taken To Heaven

And I looked, and I saw the Son of man sitting on a white cloud, with a golden crown on his head, and a sharp sickle in his hand. And another angel came out of the temple, crying with a loud voice to Jesus who was sitting on the cloud: Thrust in your sickle and reap, for the time is come for you to reap; for the harvest of the earth is ripe. And Jesus thrust in his sickle on the earth, and the earth was reaped. Rev 14:14-16 paraphrased

Behold, I show you a mystery. We will not all sleep, but we will all be changed. In a moment, in the twinkling of an eye, at the last trump; for the trumpet will sound, and the dead will be raised incorruptible, and we will be changed. For this corruptible must put on incorruption, and this mortal must put on immortality. So when this corruptible puts on incorruption, and this mortal puts on immortality, then the saying that was written will be brought to pass: Death is swallowed up in victory. O death, where is your sting? O grave, where is your victory? The sting of death is sin, and the strength of sin is the law. But give thanks to God, who gives us the victory through our Lord Jesus Christ. Therefore, my beloved brethren, be steadfast, unmovable, always abounding in the work of the Lord, because you know your labor is not in vain in the Lord. Co 15:51-58

But I would not have you to be ignorant, brethren, concerning them who are asleep, that you do not sorrow, even as others which have no hope. For if we believe that Jesus died and rose again, even so also those which sleep in Jesus, God will bring with him. For this we say to you by the word of the Lord, that we which are alive and remain unto the coming of the Lord will not prevent those who are asleep. For the Lord will come himself, he will descend from heaven with a shout, with the voice of the archangel, and with the trump of God. The dead in Christ will rise first. Then we who are alive and remain will be caught up together with them in the clouds, to meet the Lord in the air, and so shall we forever be with the Lord. 1Th 4:13-17

Those Who Are Not Saved Will Be Killed

For you will see, in those days, and in that time when I will bring again the captivity of Judah and Jerusalem, I will also gather all nations, and will bring them down into the valley of Jehoshaphat, and plead with them there. I will plead with them for my people and for my heritage Israel, whom they have scattered among the nations. They have parted my land, and they have cast lots for my people. They have given a boy for a harlot, and sold a girl for wine that they might drink. Joel 3:1-3

Yes and what have you to do with me O Tyre, Zidon, and all the coasts of Palestine? Will you give me recompense? And if you recompense me, will I swiftly and speedily return your recompense upon your own head. I will do this because you have taken my silver and my gold. You have carried my goodly pleasant things into your temples. You have also sold the children of Judah and the children of Jerusalem to the Grecians, that you might remove them far from their border. Joel 3:4-6

You will see me raise them out of the place where you have sold them, and I will return your recompense upon your own head. And I will sell your sons and your daughters into the hand of the children of Judah, and they will sell them to the Sabeans, to a people far off. For the Lord has spoken it. Joel 3:7-8

Proclaim this among the Gentiles: Prepare for war. Wake up the mighty men. Let all the men of war draw near. Let them come up. Beat your plowshares into swords and your pruning hooks into spears. Let the weak say, I am strong. Assemble yourselves and come, all you heathen. Gather yourselves together from all around. Cause your mighty ones to come down, O Lord. Let the heathen be wakened, and come up to the valley of Jehoshaphat. For there I will sit to judge all the heathen from all around. Joel 3:9-12

Put in your sickle, for the harvest is ripe. Come, go down; for the press is full, and the vats overflow. For their wickedness is great. Multitudes, multitudes in the valley of decision: for the day of the Lord is near in the valley of decision. The sun and the moon will be darkened, and the stars will withdraw their shining. The Lord will also roar out of Zion, and utter his voice from Jerusalem. The heavens and the earth will shake, but the Lord will be the hope of his people, and the strength of the children of Israel. Joel 3:13-16

And another angel came out of the temple, which is in heaven, he also having a sharp sickle. And another angel came out from the altar, which had power over fire. And he cried with a loud cry to him that had the sharp sickle, saying: Thrust in your sharp sickle, and gather the clusters of the vine of the earth; for her grapes are fully ripe. And the angel thrust in his sickle into the earth, and gathered the vine of the earth, and cast it into the great winepress of the wrath of God. And the winepress was trodden outside the city. And blood flowed out of the winepress. The flow was as high as the horse bridles, and two hundred miles long. Rev 14:17-20 paraphrased

And this will be the plague wherewith the Lord will smite all the people that have fought against Jerusalem. Their flesh will consume away while they stand on their feet, and their eyes will consume away in their holes, and their tongue will consume away in their mouth. And it will come to pass in that day, that a great tumult from the Lord will be among them. They will lay hold everyone on the hand of his neighbor and his hand will raise up against the hand of his neighbor. Judah will also fight at Jerusalem. And the wealth of all the heathen from all around will be gathered together, gold, and silver, and apparel, in great abundance. And so will be the plague of the horse, mule, camel, ass, and all the beasts that will be in these tents, as this plague. Zec 14:12-15

Jesus Treads the Winepress Alone

I have trodden the winepress alone. There weren't any other people with me: For I will tread them in mine anger, and trample them in my fury. Their blood will be sprinkled on my garments, and I will stain all my raiment: For the day of vengeance is in mine heart, and the year of my redeemed has come. And I looked, and there wasn't anyone there to help, and I wondered if there was anyone left to save. Therefore mine own arm brought salvation to me. My fury kept me strong. And I will tread down the people in mine anger, and make them drunk in my fury, and I will bring down their strength to the earth. Isa 63:3-6

The Cleansing of the Earth Begins

And I saw another sign in heaven, great and marvelous, seven angels of the Holy Spirit having the seven last plagues; for in them is filled up the wrath of God. And I saw what looked like a sea of glass mingled with fire: and them that had gotten the victory over the eighth empire, and over his image, and over his mark, and over the number of his name, standing on the sea of glass, having the harps of God. And they sang the song of Moses the servant of God and the song of the Lamb, saying: Great and marvelous are your works, Lord God Almighty. Just and true are your ways. You are the King of the saints. Who will not fear you, O Lord, and glorify your name? For only you are holy. All nations will come and worship before you, for your judgments are made manifest. Rev 15:1-4 paraphrased

And after that I looked, and saw the temple of the tabernacle of the testimony in heaven was opened. And the seven angels of the Holy Spirit came out of the temple, having the seven plagues. And they were clothed in pure and white linen that was tied breast high with a golden belt. And one of the four cherubim gave the seven angels the seven golden vials full of the wrath of God. Then the temple was filled with smoke from the glory and power of God. And no man was able to enter into the temple, till the seven plagues of the seven angels were fulfilled. Rev 15:5-8 paraphrased

And I heard God's voice out of the temple saying to the seven angels: Go your ways, and pour out the vials of the wrath of God on the earth. Rev 16:1 paraphrased

The First Vial - Grievous Sores

And the first angel went, and poured out his vial on the earth; and a noisome and grievous sore fell upon the men who had the mark of the eighth empire, and on those who worshipped his image. Rev 16:2 paraphrased

The Second Vial - All in Sea Die

And the second angel poured out his vial upon the sea; and the sea became as the blood of a dead man. And every living soul died in the sea. Rev 16:3 paraphrased

The Third Vial - Water Turns to Blood

And the third angel poured out his vial on the rivers and fountains of waters, and they turned to blood. And I heard the angel of the waters say: You are righteous, O Lord, which are, was, and will be, because you have judged thus; For they have shed the blood of saints and prophets, and you have given them blood to drink; for they are worthy. And I heard another say from out of the altar, Even so, Lord God Almighty, true and righteous are your judgments. Rev 16:4-7 paraphrased

The Fourth Vial - Sun Scorches the People

And the fourth angel poured out his vial on the sun; and power was given to him to scorch men with fire. And men were scorched with great heat, and blasphemed the name of God, which has power over these plagues: and they did not repent and give him glory. Rev 16:8-9 paraphrased

The Fifth Vial - Kingdom Full of Darkness and Pain

And the fifth angel poured out his vial on the seat of the empire; and his kingdom was full of darkness; and they gnawed their tongues for pain, and blasphemed the God of heaven because of their pains and sores, and did not repent of their deeds. Rev 16:10-11 paraphrased

The Sixth Vial - Armageddon

And the sixth angel poured out his vial on the great river Euphrates; and the water of the river was dried up, that the way of the kings of the east might be prepared. And I saw three unclean spirits like frogs come out of the mouth of the Satan, the mouth of the eighth kingdom, and the mouth of the false prophet; for they are the spirits of devils, working miracles, which go forth to the kings of the earth and the whole world, to gather them to the battle of that great day of God Almighty. Behold, I come as a thief. Blessed is he that watches, and keeps his garments, lest he walks naked, and they see his shame. And he gathered them together into a place called in the Hebrew tongue Armageddon. Rev 16:12-16 paraphrased

The Seventh Vial - It is done

And the seventh angel poured out his vial into the air; and there came a great voice out of the temple of heaven, from the throne, saying: It is done. Rev 16:17 paraphrased

And there were voices, thunders, lightning, and a great earthquake. And the earthquake was so mighty and so great, that there hasn't been an earthquake like it since men were on the earth. And the great city was divided into three parts, and the cities of the nation's fell. And the Great Babylon came into remembrance before God, to give to her the cup of the wine of the fierceness of his wrath. And every island fled away, and the mountains were not found. And there fell on men great hail out of heaven, every stone's weight was around of 56 pounds. And men cursed God because of the plague of the hail; for the plague of hail was exceeding great. Rev 16:18-21 paraphrased

Babylon the Great Will Be Judged

And there came one of the seven angels of the Holy Spirit, and talked with me, saying; Come here, I will show to you the judgment of the great whore who rules over many peoples, multitudes, nations, and tongues. With whom the kings of the earth will joined themselves to. And the inhabitants of the earth will be made drunk with the blood that they shed. Rev 17:1-2 paraphrased

So he carried me away in the spirit into the wilderness: and I saw a woman sit upon a scarlet colored beast, full of names of blasphemy, having seven heads and ten horns. And the woman was arrayed in purple and scarlet color, decked with gold and precious stones and pearls, and having a golden cup in her hand full of abominations and filthiness of her fornication. And upon her forehead was the name written, MYSTERY, BABYLON THE GREAT; THE MOTHER OF HARLOTS AND ABOMINATIONS OF THE EARTH. And I saw the woman drunk with the blood of the saints and with the blood of the martyrs of Jesus. And when I saw her, I wondered with great admiration. Rev 17:3-6 paraphrased

Satan's Eighth Kingdom

And the angel said to me: Why did you marvel? I will tell you the mystery of the woman, and the beast that carried her, which has the seven heads and ten horns. The beast that you saw was the Western Roman Empire, and then it was not an empire, and it will ascend again out of the bottomless pit, and continue until it goes into perdition. And they that live on the earth shall wonder, those whose names were not written in the book of life from the foundation of the world, when they see this Western Roman Empire that was, and is not, and yet is. Rev 17:7-8 paraphrased

And here is the mind that has wisdom. The seven heads are the seven mountains, on which the woman sits. And there are seven kingdoms: the first five kingdoms that had fallen are Babylon, Mede-Persia, Grecia, Assyria, and Egypt; as described in the Book of Daniel. The one that existed during the writing of the Book of Revelation was the sixth kingdom of the Ancient Roman Empire. And the other kingdom that had not yet come was the Western Roman Empire. When this kingdom came, it continued for a short space. This is the empire that was and then was not, and even it is the eighth kingdom, and is of the seventh kingdom, and goes into the Lake of Fire. This last kingdom is the kingdom that had the deadly wound by the sword, but still lives. Rev 17:9-11 paraphrased

And the ten horns that you saw are ten countries that have not received a kingdom as yet; but will receive power as king's one hour with the this eighth kingdom. These have one mind, and will give their power and strength to this kingdom. These will make war with Jesus, and Jesus will overcome them: for he is Lord of lords, and King of kings: and they that are with him are called, chosen, and faithful. Rev 17:12-15 paraphrased

And the ten countries that you saw on this kingdom will hate the whore, and make her desolate and naked, and will eat her flesh, and burn her with fire. For God has put in their hearts to fulfill his will, and agree to give their kingdom to the eighth kingdom, until the words of God are fulfilled. And the woman that you saw is that great city that reigned over the kings of the earth when the Book of Revelation was written. Rev 17:16-18 paraphrased

Babylon the Great is Destroyed

And after these things I saw another angel come down from heaven, having great power; and the earth was lightened with his glory. And he cried mightily with a strong voice, saying, Babylon the great has fallen. It has fallen and become the habitation of devils, and a dwelling place of every foul spirit, and a cage for every unclean and hateful bird. For all nations have drunk of the blood she shed in anger, after she joined herself together with this eighth kingdom. And the kings of the earth have also joined themselves together with this eighth kingdom with her, and their merchants of the earth have grown rich through the abundance of her delicacies. Rev 18:1-3 paraphrased

And I heard another voice from heaven, saying: Come out of her my people, so that you are not partakers of her sins, and that you do not receive of her plagues: For her sins have reached unto heaven and God has remembered her iniquities. Rev 18:4 paraphrased

Reward her even as she rewarded you, and double unto her double according to her works. In the cup, which she has filled, fill to her double. How much she has glorified herself and lived deliciously, so much torment and sorrow give her. For she says in her heart, I sit a queen, and I am no widow, and will not see any sorrow. Therefore her plagues will come in one day, death, mourning, and famine; and she will be utterly burned with fire. For strong is the Lord God who judges her. Rev 18:5-8 paraphrased

And the kings of the earth, who joined themselves to the eighth kingdom with her, and lived deliciously with her, will mourn and lament for her, when they see the smoke of her burning. Standing far off for the fear of her torment, saying: Alas, alas, that great city Babylon, that mighty city! For in one hour your judgment has come. Rev 18:9-10 paraphrased

And the merchants of the earth will weep and mourn over her. For no man buys her merchandise anymore. The merchandise of gold, silver, precious stones, pearls, fine linen, purple, silk, and scarlet; all thyine wood, all vessels of ivory and precious wood, brass, iron, marble, cinnamon, odors, ointments, frankincense, wine, oil, fine flour, wheat, beasts, sheep, horses, chariots, slaves, and souls of men. And the fruits that your soul lusted after are departed from you, and all things that were dainty and goodly are departed from you, and you will not find them anymore at all. Rev 18:11-14 paraphrased

The merchants of these things, which were made rich by her, will stand far off for the fear of her torment, weeping and wailing, and saying: Alas, alas, that great city, that was clothed in fine linen, purple, and scarlet, decked with gold, precious stones, and pearls! For in one hour your great riches have come to nothing. Every shipmaster, and all the company in ships, and sailors, and as many as trade by sea, stood far off, and cried when they saw the smoke of her burning, saying: What city can compare to this great city! And they threw dust on their heads, and cried, weeping and wailing, saying: Alas, alas, that great city, from where all were made rich that had ships in the sea by reason of her costliness! For in one hour she is made desolate. Rev 18:15-19 paraphrased

Rejoice over her, you in heaven, and you holy apostles and prophets. For God has avenged you on her. And a mighty angel took up a stone like a great millstone, and threw it into the sea, saying: Like this, with violence, that great city Babylon will be thrown down, and will not be found anymore at all. And the voice of the harpers, musicians, pipers, and trumpeters, will not be heard anymore at all in you. And no craftsman, of whatever craft he does, will be found anymore in you. And the sound of a millstone will not be heard anymore at all in you. And the light of a candle will not shine anymore at all in you. And the voice of the bridegroom and the bride will not be heard anymore at all in you. For your merchants were the great men of the earth. For by your sorceries all nations were deceived. And in her was found the blood of the prophets, and the saints, and all that were slain on the earth. Rev 18:20-24 paraphrased

Marriage Supper of the Lamb

Rejoicing over Rome

And after these things I heard a great voice of many people in heaven, saying: Alleluia; Salvation, glory, honor, and power, unto the Lord our God. For true and righteous are his judgments: For he has judged the great whore, who corrupted the earth with her union with the eighth kingdom, and has avenged the blood of his servants at her hand. And again they said Alleluia. And her smoke rose up forever and ever. Rev 19:1-3 paraphrased

Marriage of the Lamb

And the twenty-four elders and the four cherubim fell down and worshipped God, who was sitting on the throne, saying Amen, Alleluia. And a voice came out of the throne, saying: Praise our God, all you his servants, and you that fear him, both small and great. And I heard what sounded like the voice of a great multitude, and like the voice of many waters, and as the voice of mighty thundering saying, Alleluia, for the Lord God omnipotent reigns. Let us be glad and rejoice, and give honor to him: For the marriage of the Lamb has come and his wife has finished her preparation. And it was granted to her that she should be arrayed in fine linen, clean and white. For the fine linen is the righteousness of saints. Rev 19:4-8 paraphrased

Marriage Supper of the Lamb

And he said to me: Write, Blessed are those who are called to the marriage supper of the Lamb. And he said to me: These are the true sayings of God. And I fell at his feet to worship him and he said to me: See that you do not do it for I am your fellow servant, and part of your brethren who have the testimony of Jesus. Worship God. For the testimony of Jesus is the spirit of prophecy. Rev 19:9-10 paraphrased

Jesus Comes With the Saints

And I saw heaven opened, and in heaven I saw a white horse; and Jesus who sat on him was called: Faithful and True, and in righteousness he does judge and make war. His eyes were as a flame of fire, and on his head were many crowns. And he had a name written, that was known only to him. The vesture that he was wearing was dipped in blood, and his name is called The Word of God. And the armies, which were in heaven, followed him upon white horses, clothed in fine linen, white and clean. And out of his mouth goes a sharp sword, that with it he should smite the nations. And he will rule them with a rod of iron: and he did tread the winepress of the fierceness and wrath of Almighty God. And he had on his vesture and on his thigh a name written: KING OF KINGS, AND LORD OF LORDS. Rev 19:11-16 paraphrased

And Enoch also, the seventh from Adam, prophesied of these, saying, Behold, the Lord comes with ten thousands of his saints. To execute judgment upon all, and to convince all who are ungodly among them of all their ungodly deeds which they have ungodly committed, and of all their hard speeches which ungodly sinners have spoken against him. These are those who whisper and complain, walking after their own lusts. And their mouth speaks great swelling words, having men's persons in admiration because of advantage. But beloved, you remember the words that were spoken before by the apostles of our Lord Jesus Christ. How that they told you there would be mockers in the last time, who walk after their own ungodly lusts. These are they who separate themselves, sensual, not having the Spirit. Jude 1:14-19

When the Son of man does come in his glory, with all the holy angels, he will sit upon the throne of his glory. And all nations will be gathered before him. He will separate them one from another, as a shepherd divides his sheep from the goats. He will set the sheep on his right hand, but the goats on the left. Then the King will say to them on his right hand: Come, you blessed of my Father, inherit the kingdom prepared for you from the foundation of the world: For I was hungry, and you gave me meat. I was thirsty, and you gave me drink. I was a stranger, and you took me in. Naked and you clothed me. I was sick, and you visited me. I was in prison, and you came to me. Then the righteous will answer him, saying, Lord, when did we see you hungry, and fed you? Or thirsty, and gave you drink? When did we see you a stranger, and took you in? Or naked, and clothed you? Or when did we see you sick, or in prison, and came to you? And the King will answer and say to them, Verily I say to you, in as much as you have done it to one of the least of these my brethren; you have done it to me. Mt 25:31-40

Then he will say also to them on the left hand, Depart from me, you cursed, into the everlasting fire, prepared for the devil and his angels: For I was hungry, and you gave me no meat. I was thirsty, and you gave me no drink. I was a stranger, and you did not take me in. Naked and you did not clothe me. Sick, and in prison, and you did not visit me. Then they will also answer him, saying, Lord, when did we see you a stranger, or hungry, thirsty, naked, sick, or in prison, and did not minister to you? Then he will answer them, saying; Verily I say to you, in as much as you did not do it to one of the least of these, you did not do it to me. And these will go away into everlasting punishment, but the righteous will go into life eternal. Mt 25:41-46

And I saw an angel standing in the sun. And he cried with a loud voice, saying to all the fowls that fly in the midst of heaven; Come and gather yourselves together to the supper of the great God. That you may eat the flesh of kings, captains, mighty men, horses and those who sit on them, and the flesh of all men, both free and bond, small and great. And I saw the image of the eighth kingdom, and the kings of the earth with their armies, gathered together to make war against Jesus who that sat on the horse, and against his army. And the image of the eighth kingdom was taken, along with the false prophet who worked miracles before the image, which he used to deceive those who had received the mark of the beast, and those who worshipped his image. These both were cast alive into a lake of fire burning with sulfur. And the remnant was slain by Jesus who sat upon the horse with the sword that came out of his mouth. And all the fowls were filled with their flesh. Rev 19:17-21 paraphrased

Satan Chained in Bottomless Pit

And I saw an angel come down from heaven with the key of the bottomless pit and a great chain in his hand. And he laid hold on the dragon, that old serpent, which is the Devil, and Satan, and bound him a thousand years. And the angel threw him into the bottomless pit, and shut him up. Then he put a seal on him, that he should not deceive the nations anymore, until the thousand years have passed. And after that he must be released for a short time. And I saw thrones and the ones who sat on them, and judgment was given to them. And I saw the souls of the saints who were beheaded for the witness of Jesus and for the word of God, and the ones who did not worship the false prophet or his image, or receive his mark on their foreheads, or in their hands. And they lived and reigned with Christ for a thousand years. But the rest of the dead did not live again until the thousand years were finished. This is the first resurrection. Blessed and holy is he that has part in the first resurrection. On such the second death has no power, but they will be priests of God and Christ, and will rule with him a thousand years. Rev 20:1-6 paraphrased

Satan Released after the 1000 Years

And when the thousand years have expired, Satan will be released from his prison. And he will go out to deceive the nations which are in the four quarters of the earth, Gog and Magog, to gather them together to battle. The number of them will be as the sand of the sea. Rev 20:7-8 paraphrased

Followers of Satan Destroyed

And they went up covering the earth, and surrounding the camp of the saints and the beloved city. And fire came down from God out of heaven, and devoured them. And the devil that deceived them was cast into the lake of fire and sulfur, where the image of the eighth kingdom and the false prophet are, and they will be tormented day and night forever and ever. And there was not found any place for them. And I saw a great white throne, and God who sat on it, from whose face the earth and the heaven fled away. Rev 20:9-11 paraphrased

For you will see a day come that will burn like an oven. All who are proud, yes, and all that do wickedly, will be stubble. The day that comes will burn them up, says the Lord of hosts, and it will not leave them root nor branch. But to all that fear my name, the Sun of righteousness will arise with healing in his wings. You will go forth, and grow up as calves of the stall. And you will tread down the wicked. For they will be ashes under the soles of your feet in the day that I will do this, says the Lord of hosts. Remember the Law of Moses my servant, which I commanded to him in Horeb for all Israel, with the statutes and judgments. Mal 4:1-4

Judgment Seat

For we must all appear before the judgment seat of Christ. That every one may receive the things done in his body, according to what he has done, whether it is good or bad. 2Co 5:10

Then they that feared the Lord spoke often one to another. And the Lord hearkened, and heard it, and a book of remembrance was written before him for them that feared the Lord, and that thought upon his name. And they will be mine, says the Lord of hosts, in that day when I make up my jewels; and I will spare them, as a man spares his own son that serves him. Then you will return, and discern between the righteous and the wicked, between him that serves God and him that does not serve him. Mal 3:16-18

And I saw the dead, small and great, stand before God; and the books were opened. And another book was opened, which is the book of life. And the dead were judged out of those things that were written in the books, according to their works. And the sea gave up the dead that were in it; and death and hell delivered up the dead which were in them. And they were judged every man according to their works. And death and hell were cast into the lake of fire. This is the second death. And whoever was not found written in the book of life was cast into the lake of fire. Rev 20:12-15 paraphrased

New Jerusalem

And I saw a new heaven and a new earth. For the first heaven and the first earth were passed away, and there was no more sea. And I John saw the holy city, New Jerusalem, coming down from God out of heaven, prepared as a bride adorned for her husband. And I heard a great voice out of heaven saying, Behold, the tabernacle of God is with men, and he will dwell with them, and they will be his people, and God himself will be with them, and be their God. And God shall wipe away all tears from their eyes; and there will not be any more death, sorrow, crying, or pain. For the former things are passed away. Rev 21:1-4 paraphrased

And while sitting on the throne, God said, Behold, I make all things new. And he said to me, Write: for these words are true and faithful. And he said to me, It is done. I am Alpha and Omega, the beginning and the end. I will give the fountain of the water of life freely to him who is thirsty. He who overcomes will inherit all things; and I will be his God, and he will be my son. But the fearful, unbelieving, abominable, murderers, whoremongers, sorcerers, idolaters, and all liars, will have their part in the lake that burns with fire and sulfur. This is the second death. Rev 21:5-8 paraphrased

And there came to me one of the seven angels which had the seven vials full of the seven last plagues, and talked with me, saying, Come here, I will show you the bride, the Lamb's wife. And he carried me away in the spirit to a great and high mountain, and showed me that great city, the holy Jerusalem, descending out of heaven from God, Having the glory of God. And her light looked like a most precious stone, even like a jasper stone, clear as crystal. And it had a great and high wall with twelve gates, and at the gates twelve angels, and names were written on the twelve gates, which are the names of the twelve tribes of the children of Israel: On the east three gates; on the north three gates; on the south three gates; and on the west three gates. And the wall of the city had twelve foundations, and in them the names of the twelve apostles of the Lamb. Rev 21:9-14 paraphrased

And he that talked with me had a golden reed to measure the city, the gates, and its wall. And the foundation of city was square. The length was as long as the width. And he measured the city with the reed, and it measures twelve thousand furlongs (1500 miles). The length, width, and height of it are equal. And he measured the wall, and it measured a hundred and forty-four cubits (216 feet), according to the measure of a man, that is, of the angel. And the wall was made of jasper. And the city was pure gold that looked like clear glass. And the foundations of the wall of the city were garnished with all manner of precious stones. The first foundation was jasper; the second, sapphire; the third, a chalcedony; the fourth, an emerald; The fifth, sardonyx; the sixth, sardius; the seventh, chrysolyte; the eighth, beryl; the ninth, a topaz; the tenth, a chrysoprasus; the eleventh, a jacinth; the twelfth, an amethyst. And the twelve gates were twelve pearls; every several gate was of one pearl. And the street of the city was pure gold that was transparent like glass. Rev 21:15-21 paraphrased

And I did not see a temple there: Because the Lord God Almighty and the Lamb are the temple of it. And the city did not have a need for the sun or the moon to shine in it. For the glory of God shined on it, and the Lamb is the light of it. And the nations of them which are saved will walk in its light. And the kings of the earth bring their glory and honor to it. And its gates will not be shut at all by day, and there will not be any night there. And the glory and honor of the nations they will bring into it. And there will not be anything that defiles, works abomination, or makes a lie entering into it, but only those who are written in the Lamb's book of life. Rev 21:22-27 paraphrased

PART 3
THE BOOK OF DANIEL

(Chapters 7-12 paraphrased and Unsealed)

DANIEL 7

Timeline from Ancient Babylon to the End of Time

In the first year of Belshazzar king of Babylon Daniel had a dream and visions of his head upon his bed: then he wrote the dream, and told the sum of the matters. Daniel spoke and said, I saw in my vision by night, and, behold, the four winds of the heaven strove upon the great sea. And four great empires came up from the sea, diverse one from another. Daniel 7:1-3

The first great empire, Babylon (606 - 538 BC), was like a lion, and had eagle's wings, and the national symbol of Babylon was a winged lion: I beheld the king until his wings were plucked, and was lifted up from the earth, and made to stand upon his feet as a man, and a man's heart was given to it. This happened when King Nebuchadnezzar's sanity was taken away, and a beast's heart was given to him, and he was made to graze in the fields with the animals seven years. And at the end of the years, he was made to stand on his feet as a man, and a man's heart was given to him. Daniel 7:4

And behold another great empire, the Medo-Persian Empire (539-333 BC). The second was like to a bear, in that it was ferocious, but was slower in its conquest of other nations and had an enormous army. Under the Persian king Xerxes, the army numbered around 2 million men. And this bear rose itself up on one side, showing that the Persians were stronger than the Medes. And the bear had three ribs in the mouth of it between the teeth of it: and they said thus unto it, Arise, devour much flesh. The three kingdoms that they devoured were Lydia, Babylon, and Egypt; and they waged brutal military conquests, committing many atrocities, especially against the Greeks. Daniel 7:5

After this I beheld, and lo another great empire, Grecia (333-323 BC). It was swift like a leopard, and had upon the back of it four wings of a fowl, showing how Alexander the Great was swift in conquering the world in only six years; the beast also had four heads, which represented the four generals of Alexander's army; and dominion was given to it in that it was a great empire. Daniel 7:6

After this I saw in the night visions, and behold the fourth beast of the Roman Empire, dreadful and terrible, and strong exceedingly; and it had great iron teeth: it devoured and brakes in pieces, and stamped the residue with the feet of it: and it was diverse from all the beasts that were before it; and it consisted of ten kingdoms of Tripolitania, Pergamum, Macedonia, Greece, Spain, Africa, Sicily, Corsica, Sardinia, and Rome. Daniel 7:7 paraphrased

I considered the ten kingdoms, and behold, there came up among them another little kingdom called the Papal States (756-1870), and the Pope was given temporal Jurisdiction over Rome and surrounding areas. The Pope was in power when he watched three of the first ten kingdoms plucked up by the roots, and never to reappear. This was accomplished when the Rome, Sicily, and Sardinia joined themselves together and became the Kingdom of Italy. The Pope, who was the head of the Papal States, had eyes of a man, and a mouth speaking great things. Daniel 7:8 paraphrased

And I saw this kingdom of Italy remain until the thrones were cast down, and God the Father sat in judgment on his throne, whose garment was white as snow, and the hair of his head looked like pure wool: his throne was like the fiery flame and his wheels as burning fire. A fiery stream issued and came forth from before him: one million angels ministered unto him, and one hundred million stood before him: the judgment was set, and the books were opened. Daniel 7:9-10 paraphrased

I watched then because of the voice of the great words which the Pope spoke: I watched the office of the Pope remain, even until this eighth kingdom was slain, and its body destroyed, and given to the burning flame. As concerning the rest of the kingdoms, they had their dominion taken away: yet their lives were prolonged for a season and time. Daniel 7:11-12 paraphrased

I saw in the night visions, and I saw Jesus come with the angels of heaven to God the Father, and the angels brought Jesus near before him. And to Jesus was given dominion, glory, and a kingdom, that all people, nations, and languages, should serve him. His dominion is an everlasting dominion, which shall not pass away, and his kingdom is a kingdom that will not be destroyed. Daniel 7:13-14 paraphrased

I Daniel was grieved in my spirit in the midst of my body, and the visions of my head troubled me. I came near unto one of them that stood by, and asked him the truth of all this. So he told me, and made me know the interpretation of the things. These great beasts, which are four, are four great empires, which shall arise out of the earth. But the saints of the most High God shall take the kingdom, and possess the kingdom forever, even forever and ever. Daniel 7:15-18 paraphrased

Then I would know the truth of the fourth beast, the Great Roman Empire, which was diverse from all the others, exceeding dreadful, whose teeth were of iron, and his nails of brass; which devoured, brake in pieces, and stamped the residue with his feet. And of the ten kingdoms of Tripolitania, Pergamum, Macedonia, Greece, Spain, Africa, Sicily, Corsica, Sardinia, and Rome that were the head of this empire; and of the Papal States which came up, and before whom Rome, Sicily, and Sardinia fell; even of that Rome that had the Pope who had eyes, and a mouth that spoke very great things, whose look was more stout than his fellows. Daniel 7:19-20 paraphrased

I beheld, and the eighth kingdom made war with the saints, and prevailed against them; Until God the Father came; and judgment was given to the saints of the most High; and the time came that the saints possessed the kingdom. I Daniel was grieved in my spirit in the midst of my body, and the visions of my head troubled me. Daniel 7:21-22 paraphrased

Thus he said the Roman Empire shall be the fourth kingdom upon earth, which shall be diverse from all kingdoms, and shall devour the whole earth, and shall tread it down, and break it in pieces. And the ten kingdoms out of this empire are ten kingdoms that shall arise: and the Papal States shall rise after them; and it shall be diverse from the first, and shall subdue the three kingdoms of Rome, Sicily, and Sardinia. These three kingdoms were subdued when they were afraid to capture the Pope for fear of the people, and the Pope never accepted defeat. So the Pope proclaimed himself a political prisoner in the Vatican. Eventually, it became impossible for the Italian state not to recognize the independence of the Vatican, and on February 11, 1929, the Lateran Treaties established political relations between Italy and Vatican City. Daniel 7:23-24 paraphrased

And he shall speak great words against the most High, and shall wear out the saints of the most High, and think to change times and laws. And they shall be given into his hand until the last 3.5 years of time, when all the saints will be safe in heaven. Daniel 7:25 paraphrased

But the judgment shall sit, and they shall take away his dominion, to consume and to destroy it unto the end. And the kingdom and dominion, and the greatness of the kingdom under the whole heaven, shall be given to the people of the saints of the most high, whose kingdom is an everlasting kingdom, and all dominions shall serve and obey him. Hitherto is the end of the matter. As for me Daniel, my cogitations much troubled me, and my countenance changed in me: but I kept the matter in my heart. Daniel 7:26-28

DANIEL 8

Daniel's second vision

In the third year of the reign of King Belshazzar a vision appeared unto me, even unto me Daniel, after that which appeared unto me at the first. And I saw it in a vision; and when I saw it come to pass, I was at Shushan in the palace, which is in the province of Elam; and I saw in the vision that I was by the river of Ulai. Daniel 8:1-2 paraphrased

Then I lifted up mine eyes and looked, and behold there stood before the river Media-Persia which had two kings, Darius the Median and Cyrus King of Persia: and the two kings were strong; but one was stronger than the other, and the King of Persia was the stronger one, and came up last. Daniel 8:3 paraphrased

I saw Media-Persia pushing westward, and northward, and southward; so that no kingdom might stand before him, neither was there any that could deliver them out of his hand; but they did according to their will, and became great. Daniel 8:4 paraphrased

And as I was considering, behold, Grecia came from the west on the face of the whole earth, and touched not the ground: and Grecia had a great king, Alexander the Great. And Grecia came to Media-Persia, which I had seen standing before the river, and ran unto him in the fury of his power. Daniel 8:5-6 paraphrased

And I saw Grecia come close unto Media-Persia, and he was moved with choler against him, and smote Media-Persia, and defeated these two king: and there was no power in Media-Persia to stand before him, but he cast them down to the ground, and stamped upon them: and there was none that could deliver Media-Persia out of his hand. Daniel 8:7 paraphrased

Therefore Grecia grew very great: and when he was strong, Alexander the Great died; and his kingdom was divided toward the four winds of heaven, and given to Alexander's four generals: Antigonus I, Ptolemy I, Seleucus I, and Cassander. And out of one of them came forth the little kingdom of Rome, which grew into a great empire when it conquered toward the south, and toward the east, and toward the pleasant land. Daniel 8:8-9 paraphrased

And Rome grew great, even to the host of heaven; and it cast down some of the saints, even some of the disciples, to the ground and killed them. Yes, Rome magnified itself even to Jesus, the prince of the host; and they crucified Jesus, he who was the daily sacrifice; and destroyed the place of his sanctuary, which was the temple in Jerusalem. And the Scribes and Pharisee's were given to Rome to witness against Jesus. By bearing false witness, they cast down the truth to the ground; and they practiced, and prospered. Daniel 8:10-12 paraphrased

Then I heard one saint speaking, and another saint said unto the first saint who spoke: How long will be the vision concerning the death of Jesus, and of the Pharisees giving both Jerusalem and the followers of Jesus to be trodden under foot? And he said unto me: It shall be for two thousand and three hundred years; and then Jerusalem will be cleansed. Daniel 8:13-14 paraphrased

And it came to pass, when I, even I Daniel, had seen the vision, and sought for the meaning, then behold, there stood before me what looked like the appearance of a man. And I heard a man's voice come from between the banks of the Ulai River, which called and said: Gabriel, make this man to understand the vision. Daniel 8:15-16 paraphrased

So he came near where I stood: and when he came, I was afraid, and fell upon my face: but he said unto me: Understand, O son of man: for at the time of the end shall be the vision. Now as he was speaking with me, I was in a deep sleep on my face toward the ground: but he touched me, and set me upright. And he said, Behold, I will make you know what shall be in the last end of the indignation: for at the time appointed the end shall be. Daniel 8:17-19 paraphrased

The great empire which you saw which had two kings was the kingdom of Media-Persia. And the next great empire was the empire of Grecia: and Alexander the Great was the first king. Now when Alexander died, his four generals stood up in his place. And they divided the nation into four kingdoms, but none with the same power as Alexander the Great. And in the latter time of their kingdoms, when the transgressors are come to the full, a kingdom of fierce countenance, and understanding dark sentences, shall stand up. And his power shall be mighty, but not by his own power: and he shall destroy wonderfully, and shall prosper, and practice, and shall destroy the mighty and the holy people. And through his policy he shall also cause craft to prosper in his hand; and he shall magnify himself in his heart, and by peace he shall destroy many: he shall also stand up against Jesus, the Prince of princes; but he shall be broken without hand. Daniel 8:20-25 paraphrased

And the vision of the evening and the morning which was told to you is true: therefore shut up the vision; for it shall be for many years. And I Daniel fainted, and was sick certain days; afterward I rose up, and did the king's business; and I was astonished at the vision, but no one understood it. Daniel 8:26-27 paraphrased

DANIEL 9

Daniel's Prayer & Third Vision

In the first year of Darius the son of Ahasuerus, of the seed of the Medes (539/8 BCE); Darius was made king over the realm of the Chaldeans. In the first year of his reign I Daniel understood by books the number of the years; how the word of the Lord came to Jeremiah the prophet, that he would accomplish seventy years in the desolations of Jerusalem. Daniel 9:1-2 paraphrased

And I set my face unto the Lord God, to seek by prayer and supplications, with fasting, sackcloth, and ashes: And I prayed unto the Lord my God, and made my confession, and said: O Lord, the great and dreadful God, keeping the covenant and mercy to them that love him, and to them that keep his commandments; We have sinned, and have committed iniquity, and have done wickedly, and have rebelled, even by departing from your precepts and from your judgments: Neither have we hearkened unto your servants the prophets, which spoke in your name to our kings, our princes, and our fathers, and to all the people of the land. Daniel 9:3-6 paraphrased

O Lord, righteousness belongs unto thee, but unto us confusion of faces, as at this day; to the men of Judah, and to the inhabitants of Jerusalem, and unto all Israel, that are near, and that are far off, through all the countries where you have driven them, because of their trespass that they have trespassed against you. O Lord, unto us; our kings, princes, and fathers belongs confusion of face, because we have sinned against thee. Daniel 9:7-8 paraphrased

To the Lord our God belong mercies and forgiveness, though we have rebelled against him. Neither have we obeyed the voice of the Lord our God, to walk in his laws, which he set before us by his servants the prophets. Yes, all Israel have transgressed your law, even by departing, that they might not obey your voice. Therefore the curse is poured upon us, and the oath that is written in the Law of Moses the servant of God, because we have sinned against him. Daniel 9:9-11 paraphrased

And he has confirmed his words, which he spoke against us, and against our judges that judged us, by bringing upon us a great evil. For under the whole heaven there has not been done as has been done upon Jerusalem. As it is written in the Law of Moses, all this evil is come upon us: yet we did not make our prayer before the Lord our God that we might turn from our iniquities, and understand your truth. Daniel 9:12-13 paraphrased

Therefore the Lord has watched the evil, and brought it upon us. For the Lord our God is righteous in all his works that he does; for we did not obey his voice. And now, O Lord our God, that has brought your people forth out of the land of Egypt with a mighty hand, and has gotten you renown, as at this day; we have sinned, we have done wickedly. Daniel 9:14-15 paraphrased

O Lord, according to all your righteousness, I beseech you, let your anger and your fury be turned away from your city Jerusalem, your holy mountain:

because for our sins, and for the iniquities of our fathers, Jerusalem and your people are become a reproach to all that are about us. Now therefore, our God, hear the prayer of your servant, and his supplications, and cause your face to shine upon your sanctuary that is desolate, for the Lord's sake. Daniel 9:16-17 paraphrased

O my God, incline your ear and hear; open your eyes and behold our desolations, and the city which is called by your name; for we do not present our supplications before you for our righteousness, but for your great mercies. O Lord, hear; O Lord, forgive; O Lord, hearken and do; defer not, for your own sake, O my God: for your city and your people are called by your name. Daniel 9:18-19 paraphrased

And while I was speaking, praying, and confessing my sin and the sin of my people Israel, and presenting my supplication before the Lord my God for the holy mountain of my God; Yes, while I was speaking in prayer, even the man Gabriel, whom I had seen in the vision at the beginning, being caused to fly swiftly, touched me about the time of the evening oblation. Daniel 9:20-21 paraphrased

And he informed me, and talked with me, and said, O Daniel, I am now come forth to give you skill and understanding. At the beginning of your supplications the commandment came forth, and I am come to show you; for you are greatly beloved: therefore understand the matter, and consider the vision. Four hundred and ninety years are appointed to your people and upon your holy city Jerusalem, to finish their disobedience, and to make an end of sins, and to make reconciliation for injustice, and to bring in everlasting righteousness, and to seal up the vision and prophecy, and to anoint the most holy. Daniel 9:22-24 paraphrased

Know therefore and understand that from the time that Ezra leaves Babylon with the decree to build and restore Jerusalem unto Jesus, the Messiah our Prince, shall be forty nine years: and in four hundred and thirty four years the street shall be built again, and the wall, even in troublous times. And after the four hundred and thirty four years the Messiah shall be crucified, but not for himself: and the people of Satan shall come and destroy Jerusalem and the sanctuary; and its end will come at the hands of the Roman Army, and unto the end of the war, devastation and ruin are decided upon them. Daniel 9:25-26 paraphrased

And the Messiah shall confirm the new covenant with many for seven years: and in the midst of this seven year time period the Messiah shall cause the daily sacrifices of animals in the temple and the offering up of their blood to God to cease, marked by when the veil of the temple was torn in two at the death of the Messiah (Luke 23:45), and for the overspreading of abominations God will no longer reside in the temple, even until the completion of the cleansing of the sanctuary ceremony, when the seven vials that are decided upon shall be poured upon the followers of Satan. Daniel 9:27 paraphrased

DANIEL 10

Vision of Men in Linen

In the third year of Cyrus king of Persia (536/5 BC) a thing was revealed unto Daniel, whose name was called Belteshazzar; and the thing was true, but the time appointed was long: and he understood the thing, and had understanding of the vision. Daniel 10:1

In those days I Daniel was mourning three full weeks. I ate no pleasant bread, neither came flesh or wine in my mouth, neither did I anoint myself at all, till three whole weeks were fulfilled. Daniel 10:2-3

And in the twenty-fourth day of the first month, as I was by the side of the great river, which is Hiddekel; I lifted up mine eyes, and looked, and saw a certain man clothed in linen, whose loins were girded with fine gold of Uphaz: His body also was like the beryl, and his face as the appearance of lightning, and his eyes as lamps of fire, and his arms and his feet like in color to polished brass, and the voice of his words like the voice of a multitude. Daniel 10:4-6 paraphrased

And I Daniel alone saw the vision: for the men that were with me did not see the vision; but a great quaking fell upon them, so that they fled to hide themselves. Therefore I was left alone, and saw this great vision, and there remained no strength in me: for my comeliness was turned in me into corruption, and I retained no strength. Daniel 10:7-8

Yet I heard the voice of his words: and when I heard the voice of his words, then was I in a deep sleep on my face, and my face was toward the ground. And, behold, a hand touched me, which set me upon my knees and upon the palms of my hands. And he said unto me, O Daniel, a man greatly beloved, understand the words that I speak to thee, and stand upright: for unto thee am I now sent. And when he had spoken this word unto me, I stood trembling. Daniel 10:9-11 paraphrased

Then he said to me, Fear not, Daniel: for from the first day that you set your heart to understand and to chasten yourself before your God, your words were heard, and I have come for your words. But the prince of the kingdom of Persia withstood me twenty-one days: but, lo, Michael, one of the chief princes, came to help me; and I remained there with the kings of Persia. Daniel 10:12-13 paraphrased

Now I have come to make you understand what will befall your people in the latter days: for this vision is yet for many days. And when he had spoken these words to me, I set my face toward the ground, and I became dumb. And, behold, one like the similitude of the sons of men touched my lips: then I opened my mouth, and spoke, and said to him that stood before me, O my lord, by the vision my sorrows are turned upon me, and I have retained no strength. For how can this servant of my lord talk with my lord? For there remains no strength in me, neither is there breath left in me. Daniel 10:14-17

Then there came again and touched me one like the appearance of a man, and he strengthened me, And said, O man greatly beloved, fear not: peace be unto thee, be strong, yes, be strong. And when he had spoken unto me, I was strengthened and said: let my lord speak; for you have strengthened me. Daniel 10:17-19 paraphrased

Then he said: Do you know from where I came to you? And now will I return to fight with the prince of Persia: and when I am gone forth; look for the prince of Grecia shall come. But I will show you that which is noted in the scripture of truth: and there is no one that helps me in these things, but Michael your prince. Daniel 10:20-21 paraphrased

DANIEL 11

Prophecy of Battles of Great Kings

Also I in the first year of Darius the Mede, even I, stood to confirm and to strengthen him. And now will I show you the truth. Behold, there shall stand up yet three kings in Persia Cambyses (530-522), pseudo-Smerdis (522), and Darius Hystaspes, also called Darius I (522-486); and the fourth King Ahasuerus, also known as Xerxes I (486-464) shall be far richer than they all: and by his strength through his riches he shall stir up all against the realm of Grecia. Daniel 11:1-2 paraphrased

And the mighty King Alexander the Great (336-323 BC) shall stand up, and he shall rule with great dominion, and do according to his will. And when Alexander's kingdom is at its height, he will die being only thirty-three years of age, and his kingdom will be broken and divided toward the four winds of heaven. It will not be given to his heirs or the kingdom which he ruled. His kingdom will be divided up, and given to others beside these. The kingdom will be divided among his four generals - Ptolemy I, Antigonus I, Seleucus I, and Cassander. Daniel 11:3-4 paraphrased

And the king of the south Ptolemy II Philadelphus (288-285 BC) shall be strong, and one of his princes King Seleucus of Syria shall be even stronger than him, and have dominion; his dominion shall be a great dominion. Daniel 11:5 paraphrased

And in the end of years they will join themselves together; for Berenice the daughter of Ptolemy Philadelphus king of the south will come to Antiochus II Theos (261-246) the king of the north to partake in a marriage agreement. In 250 BC Antiochus will disown his first wife and married Berenice, but she will not retain the power of the arm; and he will not stand, nor his arm; for she will be given up, and they that brought her, and he that begat her, and he that strengthened her in these times. For on the death of Ptolemy Philadelphus (246 BC), Laodicea, the first and disowned wife of Antiochus, will be recalled and avenge herself by having Antiochus, Berenice, and their child put to death. Daniel 11:6 paraphrased

But out of a branch of her roots will stand up Ptolemy III Euergetes (246-221) in his estate, which will come with an army and enter into Antioch, the fortress of Seleucus II Callenicus (246-226), the king of the north, and will deal against them, and will prevail: And will also carry captives into Egypt their gods, with their princes, and with their precious vessels of silver and of gold; and Ptolemy III will continue more years than Seleucus II, the king of the north. So Ptolemy III, the king of the south, will come into his kingdom, and will return into his own land. Daniel 11:7-9 paraphrased

But his sons Seleucus III Ceraunus (226-223 BC) and Antiochus III the Great (223-) will be stirred up, and will assemble a multitude of great forces: and Antiochus III the Great will certainly come, and overflow, and pass through: then he will return, and be stirred up, even to Raphia, the fortress in southern Palestine in 217 B.C. And Ptolemy IV Philopator, the king of the south will be moved with choler, and will come forth and fight with him, even with Antiochus the king of the north, and Antiochus will set forth a great multitude; but the multitude will be given into his hand. And when Ptolemy has taken away the multitude, his heart will be lifted up; and he will kill tens of thousands: but he will not be strengthened by it. Daniel 11:10-12 paraphrased

For Antiochus the Great, the king of the north will return, and will set forth a multitude greater than the former, and will certainly come after certain years with a great army and with great riches to the battle of Paneas in 198 B.C. And in those times there will be many who will stand up against Ptolemy V Epiphanes, the king of the south: also the robbers of your people will exalt themselves to establish the vision of reviving Alexander's empire; but they shall fall. In fact, Philip V of Macedon and Antiochus made a secret pact to conquer, and share Ptolemy's overseas possessions between them. Daniel 11:13-14 paraphrased

So Antiochus the Great, the king of the north, will come and cast up a mount, and take the most fenced cities. He will take the Palestinian holdings of the Egyptians, including the key port of Sidon: and the arms of Egypt will not withstand them, neither the Jews who are his chosen people, neither will there be any strength to withstand them. But Antiochus who will come against Ptolemy will do according to his own will, and no one will stand before him: and he will stand in Israel, the glorious land, which by his hand will be consumed. Daniel 11:15-16 paraphrased

Antiochus will also set his face to enter with the strength of his whole kingdom, and upright ones with him. This Ptolemy will do: to make peace, he will give Cleopatra I, the daughter of women, to Antiochus to be his wife (192 B.C.), but she will not stand on his side or be for him. Daniel 11:17 paraphrased

After this he will turn his face to Asia Minor, and he will take many: but a Roman General named Scipio Asiaticus, for his own behalf as mediator, will cause the reproach offered by him to cease; without his own reproach he will cause it to turn upon him. Then he will turn his face toward the fort of his own land: but he will stumble and fall, and not be found. For Antiochus will perish in a fresh expedition to the east in Luristan in 187 BC. Daniel 11:18-19 paraphrased

Then Seleucus IV Philopator (187-175 B.C.) will stand up in his estate, and a raiser of taxes in the glory of the kingdom, for payments to Rome: but within few days he will be assassinated by his minister Heliodorus, neither in anger, nor in battle. Daniel 11:20 paraphrased

And in his estate will stand up, a vile person Antiochus IV Epiphanes (175-163) to whom they will not give the honor of the kingdom: but he will come in peaceably, and obtain the kingdom by flatteries: He will be very successful in battle and with the arms of a flood they will be over flown from before him, and will be broken; yes, also the prince of the covenant: For he removed the high priest Onias III, and placed Jason in his position. Daniel 11:21-22 paraphrased

And after the alliances that were made with him Antiochus will work deceitfully: for he will come up, and become strong with a small people. He will enter peaceably even upon the fattest places of the province; and he will do that which his fathers have not done, nor his fathers' fathers; he will scatter among them the prey, and spoil, and riches: yes, and he will forecast his devices against the strong holds, even for a time. Daniel 11:23-24 paraphrased

And he will stir up his power and his courage against Ptolemy VI, the king of the south, with a great army; and Ptolemy VI, the king of the south, will be stirred up to battle with a very great and mighty army; but he will not stand: for they will forecast devices against him (170 BC). Yes, they that feed of the portion of his meat shall destroy him, and his army will overflow: and many will fall down slain. Daniel 11:25-26 paraphrased

And both these kings' hearts will be to do mischief, and they will speak lies at one table. Ptolemy VI will agree to be the puppet king of Antiochus so as not to alert Rome, but it will not prosper: for yet their end will be at the time appointed. Daniel 11:27 paraphrased

Then Antiochus IV Epiphanes will return into his land with great riches; and his heart will be against the holy covenant; and he will do exploits by putting down the revolt of the Maccabees in Judaea, and then he will return to his own land. Then Alexandria will choose Ptolemy's brother Ptolemy Euergetes as King. In Antiochus' absence, the two brothers will come to an agreement to rule jointly. Daniel 11:28 paraphrased

And at the time appointed for their end, Antiochus IV Epiphanes will return, and come toward the south. In 168 BC, Antiochus will again invade and overrun all Egypt except Alexandria, but it will not be as the former or as the latter. For the ships of Rome will come against him: therefore he will be grieved, and return, and have indignation against the holy covenant. On his return from Egypt in 167 BC, he attacked Jerusalem and restored one of his officials, Menelaus, as High Priest. And he will try to Hellenized Israel by outlawing Jewish religious rites and traditions, which caused Jerusalem to be destroyed. Daniel 11:29-30 paraphrased

And the Roman Army shall be led by General Pompey; and they shall pollute the sanctuary of strength, when Pompey entered the Holy of Holies while wanting to loot the temple but found nothing. And the Romans shall take away the daily sacrifice when they crucify Jesus; and they shall place the abomination that made the Holy of Holies desolate, when the Roman procurator Valerius Gratus appointed Caiaphas as the High-Priest of the Jews (18-36 AD). Caiaphas and his counsel condemned Jesus to be crucified, and persuaded the Romans to do it. And the scribes and Pharisee's who do wickedly against the covenant shall Caiaphas corrupt by flatteries: but the people that do know their God shall be strong, and do exploits. Daniel 11:31-32 paraphrased

And they that understand among the people shall instruct many: yet they will fall by the sword, and by flame, by captivity, and by spoil, many days. Now when they shall fall, they will be helped with a little help: but they will cleave to them with flatteries. And some of them of understanding will fall, to try them, and to purge, and to make them white, even to the time of the end: because it is yet for a time appointed. Daniel 11:33-35 paraphrased

And the Roman Kings will do according to their will; and they will exalt and magnify themselves above every god, and shall speak marvelous things against the God of gods, and will prosper till the indignation is accomplished: for that that is determined shall be done. Neither will he regard the God of his fathers, nor the desire of women, nor regard any god: for he will magnify himself above all. Daniel 11:36-37 paraphrased

But in his estate he will honor the God of forces: and a god whom his fathers did not know, he will honor with gold, and silver, and with precious stones, and pleasant things. Thus he will do in the most strongholds with a strange god, whom he will acknowledge and increase with glory: and he will cause them to rule over many, and will divide the land for gain. Daniel 11:38-39 paraphrased

And at the time of the end the king of the south will push at him: and the king of the north will come against him like a whirlwind, with chariots, and with horsemen, and with many ships; and he will enter into the countries, and will overflow and pass over. He will enter also into the glorious land, and many countries will be overthrown: but these will escape out of his hand, even Edom, and Moab, and the chief of the children of Ammon (modern day Jordan). Daniel 11:40-41 paraphrased

He will stretch forth his hand also upon the countries: and the land of Egypt will not escape. But he will have power over the treasures of gold and of silver, and over all the precious things of Egypt: and the Libyans and the Ethiopians will be at his steps. Daniel 11:42-43 paraphrased

But tidings out of the east and out of the north will trouble him: therefore he will go forth with great fury to destroy and utterly to make away many. And he will plant the tabernacles of his palace between the seas in the glorious holy mountain; yet he will come to his end, and none will help him. Daniel 11:44-45 paraphrased

DANIEL 12

Prophecy of the End Times

And at that time Michael (Jesus) will stand up, the great prince which stands for the children of your people: and there will be great tribulation; a time of trouble, such as never was since there was a nation even to that same time: and at that time your people will be delivered, every one that will be found written in the book. Daniel 12:1 paraphrased

And many of them that sleep in the dust of the earth will awake, some to everlasting life, and some to shame and everlasting contempt. And they that are wise will shine as the brightness of the firmament; and they that turn many to righteousness as the stars forever and ever. But thou, O Daniel, shut up the words, and seal the book, even to the time of the end: many will run to and fro, and knowledge will be increased. Daniel 12:2-4

Then I Daniel looked, and, behold, there stood two others, one on this side of the bank of the river, and the other on that side of the bank of the river. And one said to the man clothed in linen, which was upon the waters of the river: Concerning the book of life, how long will it be between the first time the people are to be delivered, and the second time the people are to be delivered into heaven, which will be the end of these wonders? Daniel 12:5-6 paraphrased

And I heard the man clothed in linen, which was upon the waters of the river, when he held up his right hand and his left hand unto heaven, and swore by him who lives forever that it will be for three and one-half years, and 360 days there will be in each year; and when he has accomplished to scatter the power of the holy people, all these things will be finished. Daniel 12:7 paraphrased

And I heard, but I did not understand: then I said, O my Lord, what will be the end of these things? And he said: Go your way, Daniel: for the words are closed up and sealed till the time of the end. Many will be purified, and made white, and tried; but the wicked will do wickedly: and none of the wicked will understand; but the wise will understand. Daniel 12:8-10 paraphrased

And from the time that the daily sacrifice is taken away at the death of Jesus, and Papal Rule is set up in France, will be one thousand two hundred and ninety years; and 360 days there will be in each year. Papal Rule was set up after the election of King Philip in 1303 A.D.; when immediately after his election, he sent three ambassadors to the pope bearing the royal letter of congratulation. The king, while professing his obedience and devotion, recommended to the benevolence of the pope the Kingdom and Church of France. Daniel 12:11 paraphrased

Blessed is he that waits, and comes to France at the one thousand three hundred and thirty five years, when Pope Clement VI gives protection to the Jews at Avignon in 1348 A.D., when they are blamed for the black plague, and being killed because of it. But go your way till the end comes: for you will rest, and stand in your lot at the end of the days. Daniel 12:12-13 paraphrased

THE BOOK OF DANIEL TIMELINE

The Book of Daniel seems to be a contradiction of sorts. It has multiple prophecies about future events that go past Daniel's time, but the book is sealed until most of the prophecies have already come to pass, as explained below:

But thou, O Daniel, shut up the words, and seal the book, even to **the time of the end**: many shall run to and fro, and knowledge shall be increased. Daniel 12:4

The Book of Daniel was written for those who are to go through **the time of the end**. God knew that we would want to know when the world would end, and this answer is found in this book. The reason for most of this book is to build faith in Daniel. To believe future prophecy, you need to have faith in that person. What follows is a summary of the Book of Daniel, and shows us his righteousness.

Chapter 1   **Daniel kept his body holy-** Daniel didn't eat the king's meat.

Chapter 2   **Daniel reveals forgotten dreams** – Daniel revealed the dream the king forgot.

Chapter 3   **God protects the Jews** – God protected Shadrach, Meshach, and Abednego from the fiery furnace.

Chapter 4   **Daniel interprets dreams** – Daniel interprets the king's dream when his wise men of Babylon could not.

Chapter 5   **Daniel interprets visions** – Daniel interpreted the writing on the wall.

Chapter 6   **God protected Daniel** – God protected Daniel in the lions den.

Chapter 7   **Daniel has a dream** – Daniel has a dream the fall of Babylon, and the rise and fall of Media-Persia, Grecia, and the Roman Empire.

Chapter 8   **Daniel has a vision** – Daniel has a vision of the fall of Babylon, the rise and fall of Media-Persia and Grecia, and how the Roman Empire will rise out of one of the four parts of the fallen Grecia.

Chapter 9   **Daniel talks with angels** – Gabriel appears to Daniel

Chapter 10   **The powerful angel appeared to Daniel** – a power angel tells Daniel that he is to tell Daniel what is in the scripture of truth.

Chapter 11   **The powerful angel starts revelation** – the angel starts explaining the timeline prophecy.

Chapter 12   **The powerful angel finishes revelation** – the angel finishing explaining the end of time as we know it.

Daniel is a holy man physically and spiritually, and this is the type of man who wrote this book. There is another kind of faith, and it comes from fulfilled prophecy. The Book of Daniel has many prophecies that have already come to pass, and history books verify their accuracy. The reason for these past prophecies is to build faith. Knowing that all the past prophecies accurately came to pass, we can be sure the future prophecies in will also come to pass, because they are from the same prophet and the same book. What we will study next is the prophecy that has already been fulfilled.

Building the Timeline

The 70 Years Captivity In Babylon

Daniel's timeline prophecies start in chapter 9, and came about because of a prophecy from the Book of Jeremiah in chapter 25:11, as follows:

In the first year of his reign I Daniel understood by books the number of the years, whereof the word of the Lord came to Jeremiah the prophet, that he would accomplish seventy years in the desolations of Jerusalem. Daniel 9:2

And this whole land shall be a desolation, and an astonishment; and these nations shall serve the king of Babylon seventy years. Jeremiah 25:11

Daniel learned from Jeremiah that the captivity of Israel was about to end, and was praying for the nation of Israel. At the end of his prayer, Daniel was given the 70 Weeks Prophecy, which starts when the 70 years captivity of the Jews is finished.

Daniel's 70 Weeks

The Book of Daniel gives us a continuous timeline from 525 BC to the time of the end. All you have to do is unseal the prophecies. In the following prophecies that are defined by weeks, it is generally accepted that the word days in prophecy actually means years. Hindsight is 20/20, and by using the history books, the timing of these events can be verified.

The days to year's conversion in prophecy have been used before, and here are a couple examples in the following verses:

After the number of the days in which ye searched the land, even forty days, each day for a year, shall ye bear your iniquities, even forty years, and ye shall know my breach of promise. Numbers 14:34

And when thou hast accomplished them, lie again on thy right side, and thou shall bear the iniquity of the house of Judah forty days: I have appointed thee each day for a year. Ezekiel 4:6

For Daniel's prophecy timeline, one day means one year. This means that seven prophetic days are seven years, since there are seven days in a week.

So Daniels 70 weeks is in realty 70 weeks/years x 7 days in the week = 490 years.

The next step is to use this information to unseal the four verses that describe Daniel's 70 Weeks prophecy. The following verses have the verse as it is written the King James Version of the Bible first, then next is the unsealed verse with bold print. This is done to make it easy to compare the unsealed verse with the original verse, so that you can determine for yourselves that the unsealed verses are accurate.

Seventy weeks are determined upon thy people and upon thy holy city, to finish the transgression, and to make an end of sins, and to make reconciliation for iniquity, and to bring in everlasting righteousness, and to seal up the vision and prophecy, and to anoint the most holy. Daniel 9:24

Four hundred and ninety years are appointed to your people and to Jerusalem to finish their disobedience, and to make an end of sins, and to make reconciliation for injustice, and to bring in everlasting righteousness, and to seal up this vision and prophecy, and to anoint the most Holy. Daniel 9:24 paraphrased

"Know therefore and understand, that from the going forth of the commandment to restore and to build Jerusalem unto the Messiah the Prince shall be seven weeks, and threescore and two weeks: the street shall be built again, and the wall, even in troublous times." Daniel 9:25

"Know therefore and understand that from the time that Ezra leaves Babylon with the decree to build and restore Jerusalem until the coming of the Messiah the Prince will be 49 years, and 434 years: the street and the wall will be built again, even while keeping watch for attack from their enemies. Daniel 9:25 paraphrased

The going forth of the commandment to restore Jerusalem can be found in Ezra 7:7-9. This event came on the first day of the first month of the seventh year of King Artaxerxes, which would be 1 Nissan, 454 BC or March 30, 454 BC .This date marks the end of the exile of the Jews in Babylon, and the starting point for Daniel's 70 weeks prophecy. The prophecy's first part is the 7 weeks, or 49 years, which takes us up to the start of the first Jubilee. The Jubilee or the 50th year starts the 62 weeks which is the 434 years, and ends with the coming of the Messiah (49 years + 434 years=483 years).

And after threescore and two weeks shall Messiah be cut off, but not for himself: and the people of the prince that shall come shall destroy the city and the sanctuary; and the end thereof shall be with a flood, and unto the end of the war desolations are determined. Daniel 9:26

And after the 434 years the Messiah will be crucified, but not for himself: and the people of Satan, who is still to come, will destroy Jerusalem along with the sanctuary, and its end will come at the hands of the Roman army, and the godless acts will continue unto to the end of the war. Daniel 9:26 paraphrased

And he shall confirm the covenant with many for one week: and in the midst of the week he shall cause the sacrifice and the oblation to cease, and for the overspreading of abominations he shall make it desolate, even until the consummation, and that determined shall be poured upon the desolate. Daniel 9:27

And the Messiah shall confirm the new covenant (Hebrews 9:1-28) with many for seven years: and in the midst of this seven year time period the Messiah shall cause the daily sacrifices of animals in the temple and the offering up of their blood to God to cease, marked by when the veil of the temple was torn in two at the death of the Messiah (Luke 23:45), and for the overspreading of abominations God will no longer reside in the temple, even until the completion of the cleansing of the sanctuary ceremony, when the seven vials that are decided upon shall be poured upon the followers of Satan. Daniel 9:27 paraphrased

To determine the start date of these last 7 years, add the 483 years to the start date of 1 Nissan, 454 BC and you end up at the date 1 Nissan, 29 AD, which is April 1, 29 AD. In Luke 3: 1-22, it states that Jesus was baptized in the 15th year of the reign of Tiberius Caesar, His reign started in August 19, 14 AD, and gives us the range of August 20, 28 AD to August 19, 29 AD, which is within the range of the end of the 483 years prophecy.

During the final week or 7 years is when the Messiah was crucified. Christians believe that the Messiah is Jesus. We know that Jesus was crucified just before the Passover around 32 AD, and his death easily falls within the seven year prophecy. Jesus is the Messiah who fulfilled the covenant, which required the daily sacrifices and the offering up of their blood to be put on the veil before God. He did this by becoming the daily sacrifice and by offering up his life once for the sins of many. John the Baptist called Jesus the Lamb of

God, and since Jesus fulfilled this covenant as the Lamb of God, it was no longer necessary to perform this ceremony nor was it necessary for God to reside in the temple in Jerusalem.

There was another thing that happened when Jesus was crucified just before the Passover. You see, he is also the everlasting Passover Lamb of God. This is why those who are washed in the blood of the Lamb can receive eternal life, because the angel of death will Passover them. The other thing that is important about the date of the crucifying of Jesus is that it is the time of the start of 1290 day, 1335 day, and 2300 day prophecies; this start date is 13 Nissan, 32 AD, which is also April 11, 32 AD just before sundown about the ninth hour in Jerusalem.

This is where we are so far:

Hebrew Calendar	Gregorian Calendar	Other Pertinent Information
1 Nissan, 3236	3/21/524 BC Wednesday	First temple destroyed - start of 70 year prophecy
1 Nissan, 3306	3/30/454 BC Tuesday	end of 70 year prophecy - start of first 7 weeks (49 years) of the 70 weeks (490 years)
1 Nissan, 3355	3/28/405 BC Friday	end of 7 weeks (49 years) - start of 62 weeks (434 years) & first Jubilee
1 Nissan, 3789	4/01/29 AD Friday	the end of the 62 weeks (434 years) – start of 1 week (7 years)
14 Nissan, 3792	4/11/32 AD Friday	the Messiah, Gods Passover Lamb, was crucified, and died about the ninth hour
15 Nissan, 3792	4/12/32 AD Saturday	the Passover
1 Nissan, 3796	3/17/36 AD Thursday	end of 1 week (7 years) - the end of the 70 weeks prophecy (490 years)

The Birth of Jesus – around December 25, 2 BC

The infant baby Jesus was in Egypt until the death of King Herod, who died late March or early April in 1 BC.

When he arose, he took the young child and his mother by night, and departed into Egypt: And was there until the death of Herod: that it might be fulfilled which was spoken of the Lord by the prophet, saying, Out of Egypt have I called my son. Matthew 2:14-15

This helps verify that Jesus was born around December 25, 2 BC. Josephus wrote in *Antiquities of the Jews* that Herod died after a partial eclipse. Two eclipses took place in 5 BC, and one took place in 1 BC. If King Herod died in 5 BC, then this would put the birth of Jesus before April of 5 BC, which doesn't fit the known timeline of the life of Jesus. The other choice is 1 BC, which would put the birth of Jesus before April of 1 BC and does fit the timeline.

The Baptism of Jesus – April 1, 29 AD

If Jesus was born December 25, 2 BC, then his baptism was around December 25, 28 AD, because Jesus was about 30 years of age when he was baptized.

Now when all the people were baptized, it came to pass, that Jesus also being baptized, and praying, the heaven was opened, and the Holy Ghost descended in a bodily shape like a dove upon him, and a voice came from heaven, which said, Thou art my beloved Son; in thee I am well pleased. And Jesus himself began to be about thirty years of age, Luke 3:21-23

Jesus could have been baptized in the fall before December 25th or maybe in the spring the following year. We don't have an exact date, but the timelines checkpoint is 1 Nissan so this is a good bet. It doesn't seem logical that Jesus went up into the mountains for 40 days to be tempted by Satan in the middle of winter, but probably in the spring. This would give him the warmest part of the year to start his ministry.

The Crucifixion of Jesus and the taking away of the daily sacrifice – Saturday April 11, 32 AD

Then they led Jesus from Caiaphas unto the hall of judgment: and it was early; and they themselves went not into the judgment hall, lest they should be defiled; but that they might eat the Passover. John 18:28

And at the ninth hour Jesus cried with a loud voice, saying: Eloi, Eloi, lama sabachthani? Which is, being interpreted, My God, my God, why hast thou forsaken me? Mark 15:34

And now when the even was come, because it was the preparation, that is, the day before the Sabbath, Mark 15:42

And it was about the sixth hour, and there was darkness over all the earth until the ninth hour. And the sun was darkened, and the veil of the temple was rent in the midst. Luke 23-24

The ministry of Jesus is traditionally accepted as 3 to 3 ½ years. Three years if Jesus was baptized in the spring 29 AD, and 3 ½ years if he was baptized in the fall of 28 AD. Using this information, we find the date of the crucifixion of Jesus to be on Saturday April 11, 32 AD about 9 PM, just before the Passover. As we also see in Luke 23:44-45, this is the date that the daily sacrifice in the temple is taken away. This is important in that it is the starting date of the 1290, 1335, and 2300 day prophecies.

The 1290, 1335, and 2300 Days Timeline Prophecies

Before we jump into these verses, we need to cover how many days are in the prophetic year. We already determined that a week equals seven years, and a day equals one year. The prophetic year isn't the calendar year we use now, but the calendar year that God gave us in the beginning of time, and the same one that is used in the Book of Revelation.

In the Book of Revelation we are given the terms time, and times, and half a times; forty two months; a thousand two hundred and threescore days. These terms all mean 3 ½ years, but the term a thousand two hundred and threescore days tells us there are one thousand two hundred and sixty days in these 3 ½ year prophecies. This means that the prophetic calendar is a 360 day calendar (360+360+360+180=1260 days).

Many countries abandoned the 360 day calendar for some type of 365.25 day calendars, so that the seasons always came in the same month instead of slowly sliding backwards in time. There are a few calendars that still use the 360 days, but they are few. To get the right dates for these events, the 1290, 1335, and 2300 days need to be converted from the 360 day calendar into whatever calendar your country is using today. For me, it is the Gregorian calendar, and I will do these conversions for you.

THE TIMELINE CHECKPOINTS

The 1290 Days Prophecy

The starting point of these prophecies is when the daily sacrifice is taken away, and as we covered earlier, this is when the veil of the temple was torn in two from top to bottom as God left the sanctuary. This event tells us that the time of the daily sacrifice in the earthly temple is over. Jesus is the daily sacrifice in the true temple made without hands. He is the veil of the true temple and bears the sins of the world. He stands before God in heaven as a remembrance of the sins of man, like the earthly temple veil did before.

And from the time that the daily sacrifice shall be taken away, and the abomination that makes desolate set up, there shall be a thousand two hundred and ninety days. Daniel 12:11

From the time that Jesus, the true daily sacrifice, was taken away on April 11, 32 AD; until the time when the Pharisees, who are the abomination that made Jerusalem desolate, will be set-up will be 1290 prophetic years. Daniel 12:11 paraphrased

The abomination that makes desolate

Abomination definition: anything abominable; anything greatly disliked or abhorred.

Desolate definition: deprived or destitute of inhabitants; deserted; uninhabited

During the time of Jesus, the abomination that makes desolate was the Pharisees. They did not like the people following Jesus, and tried to take the focus of the people off of Jesus and onto themselves any way they could. This is both an abomination in being a detestable act, and desolate in that it made the temple and the people empty inside.

They caused the death of Jesus, because the people were following him instead of the Pharisees. Then at the death of Jesus, the temple veil was torn in two and God returned to heaven, never to return. This made the temple desolate. Then the Pharisees tried to turn the people away from Jesus and onto themselves, which is an abomination.

The 1290 Years Checkpoint – September 26, 1303

The abomination that makes desolate set up is when Pope Boniface VIII succeeded in setting up the papacy in France when he gained both spiritual and temporal power in Avignon France.

Excerpts from: http://en.wikipedia.org/wiki/Pope_Boniface_VIII

The story goes that King Philip and Pope Boniface VIII were always in conflict on one thing or another. In December of 1301, Philip was sent the Papal Bull *Ausculta fili* ("Listen, My Son"), informing Philip that "God has set popes over kings and kingdoms."

Excerpts from: http://www.newadvent.org/cathen/02429c.htm

Boniface having died, Boccasini was unanimously elected Pope, 22 October, taking the name of Benedict XI. The principal event of his pontificate was the restoration of peace with the French court. Immediately after his election Philip sent three ambassadors to the pope bearing the royal letter of congratulation. **The king, while professing his obedience and devotion, recommended to the benevolence of the pope the Kingdom and Church of France.** Benedict, judging a policy of indulgence to be necessary for the restoration of peace with the French court, absolved Philip and his subjects from the censures they had incurred and restored the king and kingdom to the rights and privileges of which they had been deprived by Boniface.

The 1335 Years Checkpoint – February 2, 1348

Blessed is he that waits, and comes to the thousand three hundred and five and thirty days. Daniel 12:12

Blessed is he that waits, and comes to the papacy at the 1335 year mark from when the daily sacrifice was taken away. Daniel 12:12 paraphrased

To get the 1335 year date, convert the 1335 years to the Gregorian calendar, and then add it to the start date of April 11, 32 AD. This will bring you to February 2, 1348. In AD 1348 - 1349, Pope Clement VI gave protection to the Jews who were being massacred during the time of the Great Pestilence, or Black Death. Clement issued Bulls for their protection and afforded them a refuge in this little State. The first massacres of the Jews in France occurred around the spring and summer of 1348. This is the blessing for the Jews who came at the 1335 years. It would be almost impossible to find the exact date for this, so this date cannot be verified. The first bull protecting the Jews was on July 6, 1948, but the protection of the Jews logically happened earlier than this, possibly on the February 2, 1348 checkpoint. If the year is the goal, then it hits it mark. If the exact date is the goal, then it may have hit the mark.

Excerpts from: http://www.historyworld.net/wrldhis/PlainTextHistories. asp?historyid=ab94

Poisoned wells: AD 1348-1349

As Europe's citizens succumb in vast numbers to the plague, a rumor spreads that the cause lies in polluted water. The wells, it is said, have been deliberately poisoned by the Jews. The first massacres of Jews occur in France in the spring and summer of 1348.

Excerpts from: **http://www.newadvent.org/cathen/04023a.htm**

Clement VI was nevertheless a protector of the oppressed and a helper of the needy. His courage and charity strikingly appeared at the time of the Great Pestilence, or Black Death, at Avignon (1348-49). **While in many places, numerous Jews were massacred by the populace as being the cause of the pestilence, Clement issued Bulls for their protection and afforded them a refuge in his little State.**

The Beginning of the End of Time

This brings us to why the Book of Daniel was written, which is the time of the end, as this verse explains:

But thou, O Daniel, shut up the words, and seal the book, even to **the time of the end**: many shall run to and fro, and knowledge shall be increased.
Daniel 12:4

And at **the time of the end** shall Egypt, the king of the south, push at him: and Syria, the king of the north, shall come against him like a whirlwind, with chariots, and with horsemen, and with many ships; and he shall enter into the countries, and shall overflow and pass over. He shall enter also into Israel, the glorious land, and many countries shall be overthrown: but modern-day Jordon shall escape out of his hand. He shall stretch forth his hand also upon the countries: and the land of Egypt shall not escape.

But he shall have power over the treasures of gold and of silver, and over all the precious things of Egypt: and the Libyans and the Ethiopians shall be at his southern border. But tidings out of the east and out of the north shall trouble him: therefore he shall go forth with great fury to destroy and utterly to make away many. And he shall plant the tabernacles of his palace between the Mediterranean and Dead seas in the glorious holy temple mount; yet he shall come to his end, and none shall help him. Daniel 11:40-45 paraphrased

The verses below explain who Egypt and Syria are attacking the son of perdition.

Now we beseech you, brethren, by the coming of our Lord Jesus Christ, and by our gathering together unto him, That ye be not soon shaken in mind, or be troubled, neither by spirit, nor by word, nor by letter as from us, as that the day of Christ is at hand. Let no man deceive you by any means: for that day shall not come, except there comes a falling away first, and that man of sin be revealed, the son of perdition; Who opposes and exalts himself above all that is called God, or that is worshipped; so that he as God sits in the temple of God, showing himself that he is God. Remember you not, that, when I was yet with you, I told you these things? And now ye know what withholds that he might be revealed in his time. For the mystery of iniquity doth already work: only he who now let's will let, until he is taken out of the way. And then shall that Wicked be revealed, whom the Lord shall consume with the spirit of his mouth, and shall destroy with the brightness of his coming: Even him, whose coming is after the working of Satan with all power and signs and lying wonders, And with all deceivableness of unrighteousness in them that perish; because they received not the love of the truth, that they might be saved. And for this cause God shall send them strong delusion, that they should believe a lie: That they all might be damned who believed not the truth, but had pleasure in unrighteousness. 2Thessalonians 2:1-12

Nuclear War

And at that time shall Michael stand up, the great prince who stands for the children of thy people: and there shall be a time of trouble, such as never was since there was a nation even to that same time: and at that time thy people shall be delivered, every one that shall be found written in the book. And many of them that sleep in the dust of the earth shall awake, some to everlasting life, and some to shame and everlasting contempt. And they that are wise shall shine as the brightness of the firmament; and they that turn many to righteousness as the stars for ever and ever. Daniel 12:1-3

The End Of Time As We Know It

These verses explain that there will be 2300 prophetic years between the death of Jesus, and the time of the end. The first is the King James Version, and the second is the same verses that are paraphrased.

Yea, he magnified himself even to the prince of the host, and by him the daily sacrifice was taken away, and the place of his sanctuary was cast down. And a host was given him against the daily sacrifice by reason of transgression, and it cast down the truth to the ground; and it practiced, and prospered. Then I heard one saint speaking, and another saint said unto that certain saint which spoke, How long shall be the vision concerning the daily sacrifice, and the transgression of desolation, to give both the sanctuary and the host to be trodden under foot? And he said unto me: Unto two thousand and three hundred days; then shall the sanctuary be cleansed. Daniel 8:11-14

Yes, the son of perdition magnified himself even to Jesus, the prince of the Jews. And by him, the need for the daily sacrifice was taken away when they crucified Jesus, and the place of his sanctuary was cast down. And the Pharisees were given to him to oppose the Lamb of God by reason of transgression, and it cast down the truth to the ground; and it practiced, and prospered. Then I heard one saint speaking, and another saint said unto that certain saint which spoke: How long shall be the vision that starts with the death of Jesus, and the Pharisees transgression of desolation; **to give both the sanctuary and the Jews to be trodden under foot**? And he said unto me: Unto two thousand and three hundred days; **then shall the sanctuary be cleansed**. Daniel 8:11-14 paraphrased

What the end of these verses is saying is that: from the time that the Pharisees caused Jesus to be crucified, because of their transgression of desolation that allowed the sanctuary and the Jews will be trodden under foot, to the time that the sanctuary will be cleansed, will be 2300 prophetic years. I believe all know the story of Jesus and who caused his death, which is the starting point. A reference to the Jews being trodden under foot is found in the Book of Revelation, as explained by the verses below:

And there was given me a reed like unto a rod: and the angel stood, saying, Rise, and measure the temple of God, and the altar, and them that worship therein. But the court which is without the temple leave out, and measure it not; for it is given unto the Gentiles: and **the holy city shall they tread under foot** forty and two months. Revelation 11:1-2

Then shall the sanctuary be cleansed is reference to the Book of Revelation, which describes the cleansing of the sanctuary ceremony during the time of the end. This writing assumes that "then shall the sanctuary be cleansed" means that this is the end of the ceremony, and marks the end of life as we know it. It is possible that it means some other point in the ceremony, it's not entirely clear. If this is referring to when Jesus cleansed the city of Jerusalem during the sixth trumpet, the timeline will need to be adjusted.

The Last 7 Years of the Book Of Revelation

This is where the last seven years of the 2300 years prophecy are described in the Book of Revelation. The verses below describes the first 3.5 prophetic years.

And I will give power unto my two witnesses, and they shall prophesy a thousand two hundred and threescore days, clothed in sackcloth. And when they shall have finished their testimony, the beast that ascended out of the bottomless pit shall make war against them, and shall overcome them, and kill them. Revelation 11:3, 7

The verses below describes the last 3.5 prophetic years of the 2300 years prophecy.

And I stood upon the sand of the sea, and saw a beast rise up out of the sea, having seven heads and ten horns, and upon his horns ten crowns, and upon his heads the name of blasphemy. And there was given unto him a mouth speaking great things and blasphemies; and power was given unto him to continue forty and two months. Revelation 13:1, 5

The date of the end of time is March 28, 2299. When you subtract 3.5 prophetic years from this end of time date you get October 16, 2295, which is the date of the second return of Jesus. When you subtract 7 prophetic years from the end of time on March 28, 2299, you get May 5, 2292, which is the first return of Jesus. This information if for those who are living during the time of the end, so they can be prepared for what is to come.

Summary

Christ death	April 11, 32 AD (Friday)	Jesus Crucifixion
1290 Years	September 26, 1303 (Thursday)	Papacy set up as spiritual and temporal power in France
1335 Years	February 2, 1348 (Saturday)	Papacy gives protection to the Jews blamed for Black Death plague
Start of Last 7 years	May 5, 2292 (Thursday)	the sixth seal, nuclear war, first return of Jesus to take saints countdown
Midpoint of 7 years	October 16, 2295 (Wednesday)	last trumpet, second return of Jesus to takes saints to heaven
End of 2300 years	March 28, 2299 (Tuesday)	last vial, end of the cleansing of the sanctuary, third return of Jesus for the marriage supper of the Lamb